SURPRISE SURPRISE

SURPRISE
A Walk of Faith Through a High Tech Industry
SURPRISE

RJ THEISS

TATE PUBLISHING
AND ENTERPRISES, LLC

Surprise Surprise
Copyright © 2012 by R J Theiss. All rights reserved.

No part of this publication may be reproduced, stored in a retrieval system or transmitted in any way by any means, electronic, mechanical, photocopy, recording or otherwise without the prior permission of the author except as provided by USA copyright law.

This book is designed to provide accurate and authoritative information with regard to the subject matter covered. This information is given with the understanding that neither the author nor Tate Publishing, LLC is engaged in rendering legal, professional advice. Since the details of your situation are fact dependent, you should additionally seek the services of a competent professional.

The opinions expressed by the author are not necessarily those of Tate Publishing, LLC.

Published by Tate Publishing & Enterprises, LLC
127 E. Trade Center Terrace | Mustang, Oklahoma 73064 USA
1.888.361.9473 | www.tatepublishing.com

Tate Publishing is committed to excellence in the publishing industry. The company reflects the philosophy established by the founders, based on Psalm 68:11,
"The Lord gave the word and great was the company of those who published it."

Book design copyright © 2012 by Tate Publishing, LLC. All rights reserved.
Cover design by Kristen Verser
Interior design by Sarah Kirchen
Photos courtesey of the Theiss Aviation Photo Collection
TIC photo by permission of Matthew Birch-Orbital Research Inc.

Published in the United States of America

ISBN: 978-1-61862-721-6
1. Biography & Autobiography / Personal
2. Biography & Autobiography / Science & Technology
12.03.23

To my wife, Hope: Shawn's mother, manager of home, office, studio, stage, Secretary/Treasurer of Theiss Aviation, Inc., and for endless hours at the computer for this writing. Thanks Honey!

ACKNOWLEDGEMENTS

Our dearest friend, Pat Williams, for her time and support during some three and a half years of editing and scripting.

Pastor Mark Headland for his many factory visits and hands-on prayers on behalf of our flying products and activities.

Theresa Gray, for her love and patience as a typist during the completion of this book.

Sister Michelle for bringing the technical elements together.

And to those blessed professional members of Tate Publishing: Stacey Baker for acceptance, Kathleen Dupre, Cassie Gray, Kristen Verser, Lauren Downen, Sarah Kirchen, etc., without whom this story could not have been properly published. My most sincere respect, love, and thanks!

TABLE OF CONTENTS

Foreword 11

Surprise, Surprise! 13

The Formative Years 19

The Disney Years 25

Post-Disney Years 33

The Adolescent Years (In Name Only) 37

World Wide Influence 51

Laying the Foundation for a New Direction ... 63

The Dawn of a New Day 81

Let It Snow! Let It Snow! Let It Snow! 89

Location, Location, Location 93

God's Plan 99

Off in a New Direction 105

A Family Affair 123

Now Was His Perfect Time! 131

A Changed World 137

Rubbing Elbows with the Big Boys. 145

A Foot in the Door. 155

Time to Reflect. 163

When It Rains, It Pours! 167

Stretched Thin 181

Fast Forward 189

Open Doors—Closed Doors. 195

The Last Days 205

All Things Considered 213

FOREWORD

We dream we can soar in our chosen realm, knowing it will take maximum passion, faith, and such daring. But who's going to lead the formation? The true story you are about to read will give you some important answers. It will give you Shawn Theiss. My late husband, an Army Flight Surgeon, Colonel Robert E. Williams, and I met the Theiss Aviation Team in 1989 shortly after moving from Colorado to Salem, Ohio. My husband had what I call the "Aviation Gene." Very few have it, let alone comprehend it. Robert immediately recognized it in Shawn. The source of Shawn's inheritance of the gene was quite obvious. We were actually taken aback (a rare state for level-headed, collected Robert), and delighted that one so young could possess such knowledge and perception concerning all things aviation. The encounter would lead to a lifelong friendship (sadly cut short in 2003 for Robert due to ALS, which he contracted during his Mount St. Helens helicopter rescue work in 1980). It didn't take us long to realize we were beholding far more than an aviation prodigy. This young aviator had a profound faith that steered his course twenty-four-seven. Those qualities of creativity, an understanding of air and space few will ever know, a boundless musicality, a seasoned intelligence far beyond his years, a gregarious sense of fun and joy, an unwavering devotion to family, a work ethic that wouldn't quit, and deep, deep compassion for all those who came his way—these all came from, and belonged to, his God. We saw that his God was always there no matter the trauma or the triumph.

Colonel Williams had a favorite quote by Barbara J. Winter:

> When you come to the edge
>
> Of all the light you know,
>
> And are about to step off
>
> Into the darkness of the Unknown,
>
> Faith is knowing one of two things
>
> Will happen: There will be
>
> Something solid to stand on
>
> Or you will be taught how to fly.

I invite you to find out what Shawn found out, to share in a life like no other you have encountered. Be prepared to be lifted up—and to soar.

—Patricia Badia Williams, M.A., NCC
Author, Educator, and Counselor
West Linn, Oregon

SURPRISE, SURPRISE!

As I start this writing, and having spent some time in the study of the Bible's Book of Revelation, I can't help but wonder if anyone will be around to read it, or for that matter, even have time to look into it. Then too, it may be that the one I seek to honor will be the target of hate or harm considering the attitude of many towards Christians in this day and age.

Having prayed about this effort, if it were not published, I would have failed to share the workings of an all powerful and exacting God in the life of one person, who, from an early age, learned to look to and depend upon the Creator of all for all of his earthly needs.

The sex of the unborn child was a mystery before its birth in 1972.

The monumental event was also a mystery to the parents-to-be as they had been assured long before that the addition of a fourth child to the family could never be.

The dark-haired, round-faced, little fellow was born amid family controversy—how to spell the newborn's name. His Mother wanted his name to be spelled Sean (easily mispronounced as seen). The family name Theiss (pronounced tice), was of German origin and was constantly mispronounced by all as theese, thise, tha-is, etc. Dad Theiss simply did not want his son to have a lifetime of being referred to as "Seen Theese." The name was to be spelled Shawn, and it stuck.

Shawn's mother, being of French origin, announced his middle name to be Maurice; it stuck. And so, properly labeled, the new child assumed his place in the Theiss family.

Being twelve years the youngest sibling had its advantages—at first. At age five, when his siblings were seventeen, eighteen, and nineteen, his family position had suddenly changed from "lil' darling" to "spoiled brat!" Being locked out of bedrooms was bad enough, but the location of the family home (some four miles south of Fort Myers, Florida) provided Shawn with no other children for playmates. A pony, dog, two ducks, a hamster, and his eldest brother's pet snake were it.

His adults-only association for most of his first five years led to an obvious dislike of the actions of others his own age. They were too childish. The first attempt to register him with the YWCA pre-school program resulted in his fastening himself firmly under the cars dash panel. Extraction came about at his mother's office, only when he was convinced that the "pre-school threat" had passed. Sometime later, Shawn did agree to spend his mornings at the YWCA, after his being allowed to ride herd over a few of the other children in attendance.

Shawn's rather unique social attitude (for his age) yielded a unique use of the English language; his sentence structure and expressions were that of an adult. It should also be said that his lack of patience at times was not easy to take by his elders.

How could a youngster such as this make it through the day without a black eye or bloody nose? He did so by being a charmer among adults and a diplomat with other children. Often, when introduced to adults, he was the first to offer his hand to the men, and surprised many a lady with the kissing of the back of their extended hand.

In the beginning, he could sound so authoritative when speaking with other children they generally bought his offerings—hook, line, and sinker. Often it was said by family that Shawn was born at age forty-two.

Firmly set in the minds of the Theiss children were the facts of their Christian faith. Sunday was for church going, not working. Wednesday was Bible study evening, and prayers were always offered before eating and at bedtime. All seemed to have meaning to little Shawn, although it was hard for him to sit still for any length of time in church. This from a very early age, according to a doctor friend of the family, was the result of his being hyperactive. The popular cure for that day was Ritalin, a drug prescribed for hyperactive children that gave parents some rest while turning the child into a mind-numbed robot.

Hope would have none of it, and after consulting with a Canadian doctor, put the entire family on a special diet. While they still ate well, the new diet made Shawn much calmer in his day to day activities. Unfortunately, even though the school system was notified, it was easy to know when a birthday of another child was celebrated in class. The sugar cookies and Kool-Aid had Shawn climbing the walls for hours after he got home. During the next several years, the family prayer was for Shawn to grow out of the hyper condition without the adverse effects of the drug that was rather devastating to those in their early teens who had become hooked at the convenience of their parents.

In retrospect, one of the most profound decisions by Shawn's mother would take place at the age of six and would remain in effect for much of his life. "Honey, I'm with Shawn all day long, every day, and I think it would be good for the both of you if you were to spend the last hour of the day together." Good idea? Profound!

The last hour was generally spent in bed and was looked forward to by both father and son. It was a time for storytelling, which called for some effort on Dad's part. There was a new story required for each evening in the week—spring, summer, fall, and winter. And each Memorial Day, Fourth of July, Labor Day, Halloween, Thanksgiving, Christmas, Valentine's Day, and Easter. By request were the many airplane stories. Having flown since 1946, Dad had plenty to tell. In addition to stories were the times for just plain talking about daily activities, happenings at school, and, always questions about God, Jesus, and Bible stories. It was these discussions that most probably led to Shawn's understanding of prayer and the result to be expected. Prayer was always the conclusion to the father-and-son-quality-time hour.

Shawn prayed for and expected answers to every phase of his daily experience. The best example of this was a point of embarrassment in later years. Shawn was six when the family stopped for a Bar-B-Q meal at a famous spot. Old South Bar-B-Q was located near Fort Myers Beach, Florida, and as usual, the place was packed. Prior to the stop, young Shawn had been constipated. After orders had been placed, he, by himself, suddenly took off for the men's room located at the far end of the large dining room. After being gone for some time, his mom moved to check on him. The door to the men's room flew open. While still holding the door wide, he loudly announced for all to hear "Hey Mom! Jesus healed me!"

THE FORMATIVE YEARS

Just how much one's environment has to do with the shaping of a person's interest and abilities in any area of endeavor has been a subject of controversy, which as far as I know, hasn't been pinned down to a definitive answer. On behalf of environmental influence, the following is offered.

At something less than one year old, Shawn was (on a number of occasions) bundled along with the rest of the family into an aircraft and flown to a weekend air show. There would be a car waiting for them at the airport of destination, along with the rooms and dining reservations for their stay. Most air shows were two-day events held on Saturday and Sunday.

Rain or Shine, with Capt. Kirk on stage at the airshow, it was a GO Situation.

AIR SHOW ANNOUNCERS RETURN
FOR SECOND SOUTHWEST FLORIDA
AIR EXPOSITION

Rich Theiss and Hope Trivette will once again represent some of the worlds greatest aerial acts, as they return to their home town airport for the airshow to be presented on April 23, 1972.

The announcing team, now in their 13th season usually spend their weekends in another part of the country as they narrate for thrilling airshows; however they will travel little over one mile to handle the Jaycees flying program on the 23rd.

Note the NASA two-man spacecraft display at most airshows

20 | R J THEISS

Hope introducing world famous long distance flyer, Clarence Chamberlin, to the airshow audience.

Flying trips such as this would take place as many as fifteen times during an air show season, and Shawn's parents would be narrating the entire program as they had for sixteen years. Shawn would go along with the air show team for the first five years of his life. With Mom, no child was left behind. Might this have had anything to do with his interest in flying things?

Air shows were not the only flight activity Shawn was exposed to. His mother, Hope, was a pilot as was his father, Richard, and his older brother, Marc. Sisters Cindy and Michelle, in addition to riding in the back seat, knew what was necessary to keep the family Piper Tri-Pacer in a clean and shiny condition. The "Brat" was not involved in the maintenance of the aircraft.

Shawn at the controls of his first flying creation.
Prop and wing from Cadillac engine and dash panel

Not to be outdone, Shawn had his own thing going. While others his age were content to color the drawings in coloring books, Shawn would first draw airplanes on blank paper and then add the colors. Most church services were the time and place he chose to do the drawings. It kept him busy at a time when silence was golden.

By age six, he was building model planes, but not the kind in boxes from stores. The fuselage or body was usually fashioned from toilet paper tubes with a hole cut into it, representing an open cockpit. Most of his creations had two wings made of folded paper with a balsa stick for a wing spar. To form the tail, the tube was smashed at one end to receive its paper rudder and elevator units.

Though crude in appearance, they did somewhat resemble aircraft of the 1930s and 40s. Why old double wingers? Shawn's parents were members of the Antique Aircraft Association, and Shawn was in regular attendance for all of the AAA fly-ins.

As a model plane builder, he was prolific. Model kits were not for him. Even when reproducing models of real aircraft, he preferred to build from scratch. The ceiling of his bedroom called for constant ducking by adults so as not to collide with a variety of flying things being suspended there.

Fly they must. Unlike his older brother, Marc, who had become skilled at building plastic models, Shawn required that all of his planes be perfectly balanced for flight.

Still being young, his bending and tweaking of the flying surfaces to improve the models performance gave indication that possibly a higher power had pre-planned some innate understanding of flight—for if he built it and tweaked it, it flew!

A budding knowledge of flight was not his only gift from above. His older brother, Marc, could set out a good and steady beat with drum sticks; Shawn had natural rhythm. His eldest sister, Cindy, harmonized with melody at age three and a half; his ear for music was all there. Michelle was the dancer and artist; his drawings of aircraft had good perspective.

The children's collective talents were utilized in their parent's onstage activities. Indeed, the Theiss family was close-knit as they presented "The Wee World of Theiss"; an early NBC cablevision children's program based on the characters and tales of Walt Disney Classics. The Saturday morning program originated from the studios of WMYR TV in Fort Myers, Florida.

Brad Lacy, the studio manager, suggested that the Theiss family become known to Walt Disney World. Their first visit to the Walt Disney Casting Department led to contracts for both parents. Hope, being a former professional actress, dancer, musician, model, air show performer, and announcer went with the entertainment department. Richard was destined to be with the wED Imagineering section.

On the return trip from the Orlando area, Hope stated emphatically, "Well, it's about time! After having spent our way through seven family visits to the Magic Kingdom, they can keep us for a change."

THE DISNEY YEARS

Time for a family move. Well, not all of the family. Sister, Cindy, and brother, Marc, were now married, and Michelle was soon to be. The current situation left Shawn in a somewhat enviable position. "Little King Pin on his way to Never, Never Land."

While awaiting the construction of their new Orlando home, the family occupied a second floor condo close to the Disney complex. The second floor balcony offered Shawn a new dimension in flight testing; now planes could be launched and observed for a longer period of time before coming to rest on the ground below. Though many planes were built and flown from the balcony, the most memorable was the self designed transport that Shawn flew from the balcony to the court yard below. Although the shape of the stick and tissue craft was not unusual, the pilot was. Having fashioned a tiny cloth skull cap, Shawn fastened the flight gear on to the head of his pet (a young male gerbil). The gerbil was then placed into the forward cabin area, and then flown in the model from the balcony to the smooth grass lawn below. After the plane landed, Shawn would quickly run downstairs to retrieve both pilot and plane. Much to the amazement of the witnessing neighbors, upon landing, the gerbil always disembarked and stayed close to the plane as if waiting to be retrieved for the next flight.

While his parents were with the Walt Disney Company, young Shawn was starting to give evidence of having a mechanical prowess. Tools in his hands were well placed. Over objections by his mother, Richard often took his son to the Theme Park, after hours, to help repair automated characters located in various windows through-out the complex. Shawn, still a child, could fit under the movie-themed sets, determine the problem, and with proper tools, make the repair.

In all truth, Hope, on occasion, had Shawn with her after the park was closed for parade rehearsals. The exposure to the costumed Disney characters led to Shawn's first crush on one of the opposite sex, "Alice" from the wonderland movie.

She was indeed a cutie in her blue and white dress with long blonde hair flowing. Her suspicions were confirmed when the blushing seven-year-old handed her a note that had been written on the cobble stone street. Hard to read, she did make out "I love you!" That did it! Being a dress rehearsal with only Disney employees present, she gave him her attention as her activities would permit. He was hooked. The other characters played along with the fairytale romance, which would last for the better part of the summer season.

During that time, Shawn never missed the Disney character parade. As he sat at his favorite spot along the parade route, Alice always blew kisses his way, which brought a red blush to his face and ears. The seven dwarfs, along with Tweedle Dee and Tweedle Dum, took turns in moving close enough to bend over to Shawn (so that he alone could hear) and sing the melody, "We know who you love." Three more shades of red were added to his face and ears. Only some years later did Shawn learn that the woman portraying Alice was nearly thirty years old. There is something to be said for Disney magic.

Within a relatively short span of time, the new, Orlando-area home was finished, and the family made the move from condo to house. Of course, along with household items to be moved, were the many flying models. Their new home would eventually require many holes in his bedroom ceiling for the suspending of planes yet to be built. The new garage would never see cars; both father and son were now building models together. Having settled into their new home, it was during an evening hour in bed that Shawn gazed up at the ceiling full of his handiwork and said, "Dad, when I grow up, I'm going to design and build airplanes for people." The statement was simple, straight forward, and sincere. He was ten years old.

Although in time his life would delve into TV production, radio announcing, script writing, music, aircraft, and mechanical design, all of the above were incidental to his constant striving toward a career in aviation. Along the way were the significant milestones that prepared the developing airman.

While still age ten, an aunt gave Shawn a gift from her visit to Cape Canaveral. It was a glass globe in which a solar collector cell and electric motor with a propeller was enclosed. To most, this was a very nice table display to demonstrate the concept of how solar power could be harnessed. But to Shawn, the table-top display was not the best use of this device;

it had a propeller on it; therefore, it should fly. Shawn removed the innards from the globe, used Dad's Dremel tool to grind the excess plastic from the solar collector, and designed and built a balsa plane that was to be powered by the solar unit.

It was during the bed time ritual that Dad first learned of the project in progress. Lovingly, he cautioned the youngster about being too optimistic. After all, German modelers had been trying for some time to successfully fly with solar power, and, to the elder's knowledge, it had gone nowhere.

The next day, having returned home from his Disney office, Richard was met by a very excited son. "Hey Dad, watch this!" Walking a short distance to an open field, Shawn launched the model plane. In the hot Florida sun, it flew and flew and flew. The termination of the flight was by ramming into the side of a neighboring house. Being light in structure, both plane and house survived.

First to build and fly a solar powered
model when only ten years old.

Shortly after, Model Airplane News magazine published the story and plans for Shawn's "Solar Pup." The article was shared with Dr. Paul McCreedy, who was the first man to design and fly a solar powered, human-carrying aircraft. Shawn was given credit as being the first to successfully fly a solar powered model plane.

For the last three years with the Disney Company, Richard was involved almost exclusively in aviation related events; the flying portion of the dedication of the new Orlando International Airport, the landing of both French and British Concords on parallel runways at the same time, the flying portion of the half-time program for Super Bowl XVIII, Florida Air Guard salute during the dedication of EPCOT center, and the building of the air shows for the Lakeland EAA winter fly-in events.

Although he was present for all of these flying events, Shawn especially enjoyed Lakeland's Sun-N-Fun week of activities, and why not? The old time pilots of old time aircraft (members of the AAA) took the young enthusiast under their wings (so to speak). He stayed in their trailers, ate with them, and flew in their front cockpits for most of the week. He built models of most of their planes, often giving the models to them as gifts.

The AAA (Antique Aircraft Association) would observe the Sabbath day with a church service, usually held in one of the nearby hangers. Much to the surprise and delight of all in attendance one Sunday, Shawn volunteered to offer opening prayer. Especially appreciated was the petition for the safety of all who would be flying aircraft that day. He was eleven years old.

Shawn, as a Disney toy soldier. Disney parade float in background.

For some time, Shawn was developing his gift of an ear for music. Within a very short time, he mastered any toy instrument he could get his hands on—an ability that led to his winning first place in a Disney Halloween contest dressed as a toy soldier. He went on to win first place for the next two years. There were, on average, 150 or more contestants each year that entered in the event. The final win found Shawn dressed as the Red Baron, complete with a cardboard Fokker Tri-Plane and flying suit of the period.

The Red Baron. Ready for takeoff.

As for the building of model planes during the later days at Disney, Shawn and his Dad were involved with both the building and flying of indoor and outdoor, free-flight, scale aircraft. Still getting together at bedtime, the father/son team was also enjoying many free time hours in the garage workshop. At least Hope knew at most times what her two male charges were up too.

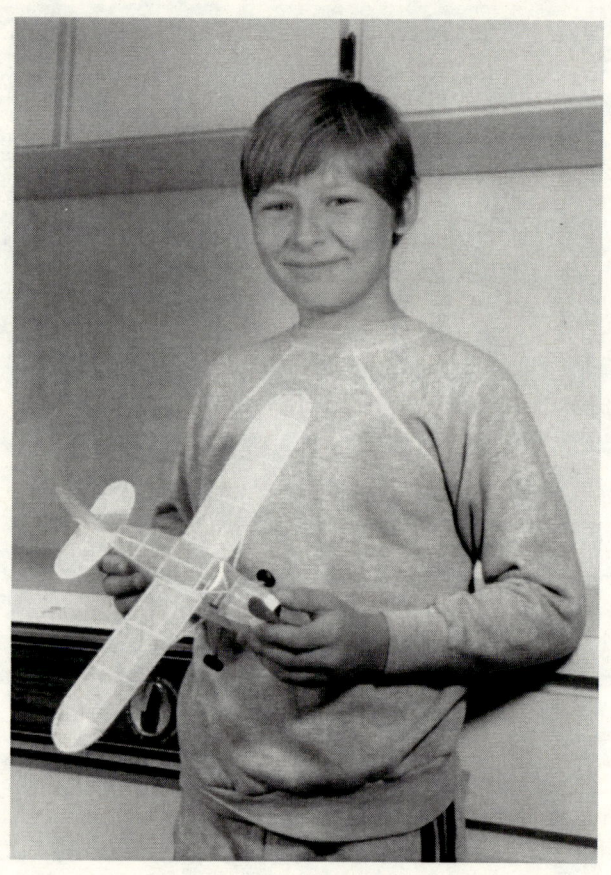

This one really flies!

POST-DISNEY YEARS

As with all good things, Disney too, came to an end. Still being young, Shawn had nothing to do with the internal circumstances that led the company to lay off thirty-five vice presidents and a host of highly paid employees. All he knew was that the family would be moving to Connecticut, where Dad would be joining a division of Warner Brothers Studios.

One of the severed Disney Vice Presidents, Dave Ginginbach, was now heading up the Warner Brothers division that was concerned with three dimensional characters as part of entertainment for a chain of restaurants called Gadgets. Their biggest competition at that time was a pizza house for young families named Chuck-E-Cheese. Although Gadgets has long been gone, Chuck-E-Cheese is still going strong.

In preparation for the move to Connecticut, a call was placed to Shawn's eldest sister, Cindy. She and her husband, Blaine, were currently living in Naugatuck, a town some ten miles from the Warner Brother's complex. At that time, Blaine was managing the Southbury Racquet Club and could be counted upon to help unload the moving truck and trailers being transferred by Mom and Dad.

It might be mentioned here that the Richard Theiss family, to the person, had the most unusual ability to laugh at themselves for the many flat-out stupid things they were included in from day to day. Indeed, family get-togethers always featured a "hoot session" listing the latest to occur in each family branch.

Still a source of family laughter was the move itself from the Orlando area to Middlebury, Connecticut. Shawn would be traveling with Dad in the largest U-Haul truck available with the largest U-Haul trailer in tow.

His mother would follow in the family car, again with another large trailer in tow. Actually, the trailer being much too large and heavy for the car. Shawn's mother would encounter one of the most miserable road trips of her life (to that time).

All seemed to be going well from Florida to New Jersey, where the convoy of two vehicles came upon the "Garden State Parkway." Both having passed through the ticket booth, it soon became evident that Hope was no longer following Dad and Shawn in the truck. In fact, within a few miles she was seen in a lane of traffic going in the opposite direction. As soon as a crossover was found, the truck was turned around so as to follow the small red car with the large white trailer in tow. Again, the now confused driver of the car was spotted, again in a distant lane moving in the opposite direction.

Having had enough of the merry-go-round stuff, it was quickly decided that Mom was wrong and would, surely, soon be following them toward the North again. Over an hour had passed, and of all the many cars around them, father and son had not again seen the family car. Where on earth could she be?

"Hey, Dad!" Shawn went on to ask, "Have you noticed that we are the only truck around?"

"No!" was the response of the moment. However, all of a sudden, a lot of things were starting to make sense to both of them like the sign way back that stated cars only and the agents who seemed to be trying to get their attention at every series of ticket booths as they dropped a quarter in the slot— 25 cents for cars. Good grief! Could they be on the wrong highway?

Then, there appeared a large road side sign—State Highway Patrol Station, One mile on right.

Now, visibly nervous, Richard, with deft purpose, cut off a few cars as he drove into the parking lot at the front of the State Highway barracks.

Upon entering, a lone State Trooper was found at a desk to the rear of the office complex. "Look," the stunned officer offered, "I have no idea of how you made it this far on an auto only roadway, but you only have three more gates to get through. So, if I were you, I'd go through the farthest gate on your left and try to make it all the way out. If you're stopped, I haven't seen you. Got it?"

The word had passed up the line of toll booths and, although agents were making an effort to stop the truck, Dad and Shawn breathed a sigh of relief as they pulled away from the last booth, after having left the price of a car in every booth along the entire length of the parkway.

A weary Mom Theiss was shocked to see the U-Haul truck pull up in the parking lot of Patty's Pantry, a pre-determined meeting location. The last she had seen of it was in the State Highway Patrol parking lot; reason enough to assume the worst.

The next day found the Theiss belongings being unloaded into the family's new, northern house. A small group of neighborhood children had gathered to check out the new kid in the area. Shawn was busy with his moving of what seemed to be an endless armful of model airplanes.

Finally, upon unloading the last of his models and modeling supplies, he stopped long enough to shock all (young and old) with a seemingly simple question, "Hey, does anyone know where I can get some dope?"

From the moment of dead silence came the bursting voice of his sister Cindy, "He means paint. That's what they call airplane paint—dope. You know—red, green, blue!" After another moment of silence and awkward looks, it was evident to Dad that those present hadn't a clue. "My goodness," he thought, "How things have changed."

One thing hadn't changed for Shawn. He was quick to realize that the low flying aircraft overhead were landing at an airfield nearby. In fact, the glide path was right over his house. Wow, this was going to be a neat place to live.

THE ADOLESCENT YEARS (IN NAME ONLY)

Shawn's first summer in Connecticut was a busy one. Between his daily visits to the local airport, less than five minutes away by bike, he had started his first large airplane project. A neighbor had torn down an old garage and had given Shawn a dozen or so planks. With hammer in hand, he fashioned a fuselage large enough to sit in. For more than a month, the twelve-year-old spent many an hour peering over the edge of his cockpit. Without a doubt, his imagination had him flying high over the northern landscape. He never once feared becoming lost. For there, mounted on the dash panel, was his trusty compass—a gift from one of his new middle school teachers.

Shawn's project shared the basement with another project, an antique sleigh his mother had bought for his Dad. Both labored long hours into the winter season, until Shawn flatly stated, "Dad, that thing will never fly!" He continued, "Know what I want for Christmas? One inch square strips of wood, maybe fifteen feet long, and some thin ply for gussets. Oh! And some good glue too!"

That following Christmas morning found Shawn's major gifts too large to fit under the tree. In his mind, Shawn had already begun to design an airplane indicative of the craft he had been raised around. However, this project would require more space than afforded in the basement. No, the double winged, tandem cockpit project now required the garage. The family cars went out.

Some months later, Shawn brought one of his friends from the local airport to see the completely framed fuselage. The gentleman was the local FAA examiner. As the man was leaving, after having spent some time discussing the craft with Shawn, Shawn's mother (speaking too softly for her son to hear) said, "He really thinks it will fly." The response of the examiner was not what the mother had in mind. "Well," he stated, "if he builds the rest of it as well as this fuselage, I'm afraid it will." Fortunately for his mother's nerves, the project was never finished due to damage that would be sustained during the next family move (yet to come).

Shawn Theiss checks over the aircraft he designed and is building himself.

Little did Shawn's mother realize that this was only the start of a lifetime of concern over his flight activities. Indeed, there would be many hours spent on her knees. This would keep her sane and him safe.

Of course, there seemed to be an up-side to Shawn's aviation activities. His longer periods of concentration gave indication of the young airman growing out of the hyperactive condition that had plagued his early years. God does indeed answer the prayers of concerned, loving parents.

During the two years of Shawn's middle school education, it became obvious to his parents that studies of interest were sure to bring good grades. However, no interest and little effort resulted in squeak-by marks. Homework was not easily focused on. On the other hand, his free time activities excelled. Weekends usually involved an indoor or outdoor model plane meet somewhere in the northeast.

One of Shawn's giant scale rubber band powered model designs.

An old-time, free-flight event at the Carstens Publishing Company located in northeastern New Jersey found Shawn high in a tree that had captured one of the older contestant's model. Richard was slightly concerned as Shawn quickly made his way to the stranded aircraft and back down again. "Ah, Dad, it wasn't any big deal," was Shawn's response to Dad's concern about climbing the tree. However, this would not be the last time that the boy's agility would surprise dad. His retrieval of the six-foot, spanned craft without a scratch earned the agile youngster a gift of a .020 gas class *Miss America*. The model was probably the only kit that Shawn built without changing the construction plans. The budding designer in him usually called for at least one major modification per craft. Two years later, the blue and yellow plane took first place at the S A.M. Nationals at Andover field in upper New York State in the senior division; Shawn was fourteen years old at the time.

The national champ with gas powered "Miss America."

With Shawn about to begin high school, the Theiss family decided that a new home was in order; one closer to the high school of choice and a little more rural. A home was found in the hills of Washington, Connecticut, on the side of a heavily wooded mountain. The mountain was named Ararat Mountain, and, ironically enough, the home was a very modern, flat-roofed design (actually designed by students of the famed Frank Lloyd Wright) that could have easily resembled the biblical Noah's Ark. Nonetheless, the home had a certain charm about it that appealed to the family. So with contracts signed, the Theiss family made yet another move to a new home.

As with most high school freshman, Shawn was about to broaden his life experience. So too, would it be with his parents.

Only too clearly could Richard and Hope remember when Shawn's sister, Michelle, was a teenager. She (as with Shawn) was quite the precocious young person. Her mature appearance and actions garnered the attention of many a young man. "Good Heavens!" thought Shawn's parents. "Will it be a thing with girls this time? And at our ages?"

As it turned out, Shawn's mature, older actions were attracting more mature (and somewhat older) girls. They most certainly did not look to be close to his age, and their manner of dress... things could get testy around the house!

Heaven only knows where his private life might have gone had not some of the older interested girls confided in mom Theiss. Thinking back in time, Hope handled herself well. Rather than land on him with both feet, she chose to simply monitor all of his activities much more closely.

As far as Shawn's social life in and around Shepaugh High School, a parent-teacher meeting revealed Shawn to be a bit of a loner. There was a pizza parlor in town where most of the local kids would gather after school to gossip, flirt, and generally engage in the typical teenage antics of the day. Shawn, however, rarely joined in the frivolity. Instead, he preferred to rush home from school to work on his planes.

Loner or not around his High School, Shawn's aviation focused after school activities most probably accounted for his dating the girls from the local church fellowship, and, even they were subject to the priority of his first love… airplanes! Many were the dates that were cancelled because of a conflict with a model airplane meet.

Of comfort to his parents were the ongoing father-son bed time conversations that revealed Shawn's female interests, and the fact that God was indeed with Shawn during the times they could not be.

The spring season of his first high school year brought a pleasant surprise to Richard. Shawn had gone out for track. He would be a dash man and do the hurdles and long jump—the very same events his Dad competed in many years before. As a result of his new found sport, Shawn's days of being a loner were gone forever. Former track record times and distances were being reset by Shawn each of the three following years of school. Though not a loner anymore, Shawn would find time to pray alone before every track meet. While his track buddies were listening to music, singing, laughing, and joking on the way to the various meets, Shawn would quietly put his track jacket hood over his head, slip down in his bus seat, and pray.

In his junior year, he would long jump far enough to go beyond the saw dust pit (he sprained both ankles on that one)! Later, as the senior season closed, he found himself as the Regional Champion in the 110 yard high hurdles and the Connecticut State Champion in the three hundred yard intermediate hurdles.

As it approached, Richard knew that the state event was the most important of Shawn's high school track career; not only to Shawn, but also to his coach, team mates, and of course his current girlfriend.

As he watched Shawn move into the starting blocks, dad Theiss was most aware of the pressure Shawn was feeling in the pit of his stomach; the elder Theiss had been there. Yet, dad was not aware of the athlete prancing and boasting aloud in the lane next to Shawn.

Big mistake! Shawn performed well under pressure, and was known to take down the boastful!

While in the starting stance, Shawn's breathing was slow and his body was relaxed; his bowed head was of purpose… he was praying. When Shawn prayed, his expectations were high, and when his expectations were high… "Runners ready… set…" The starting gun fired, giving cue to the roar of the crowd. In that instant, all that had been relaxed and calm within Shawn's body, now exploded forth with every ounce of energy available!

The final heat of the most strenuous event was on its way, and Shawn was neck and neck with the big boaster.

The other six were close on their heals. 50 meters down, and Shawn had settled into an aggressive lead pace. 150 meters, and the pack had now started to thin out. Ahead lay the 200 meter mark; the preverbal "wall" that every hurdler dreaded. This was the point were your muscles began to burn, where your breathing and hurdle form became more difficult to maintain, and the point where many runners would simply run out of steam!

Teachers, friends, and parents were vocally pulling for their favorite, but Richard was silent. It was his turn to pray, and pray he did. All the former races through all of the former years were wrapped into this one final event, and Richard found himself overloaded with concern for his son. "Had he expended too much energy in the High Hurdles event? Had his ankles been weakened during the long jump? Should the coach have pulled him from the relay race to allow ample rest for this event?" Slowly dad raised his head to check on Shawn's progress.

His first outburst was a resounding "Yes!" as he watched Shawn cross the finish line… a full hurdle length ahead of the nearest competitor! As Shawn slowly walked back towards the cheering crowd, he spotted his father in the grandstands and pointed towards Heaven, signifying that Jesus had been responsible for the win. His pre-event prayer had once again been answered; to God be the glory!

Scholastically, his best subject of study was (as might be expected) drafting design. He was always first to finish with the required drawings so as to spend time on a new airplane drawing. As his instructor once told his father, "I can't fault Shawn for his extra classroom drawings. His work is perfect!" Shawn would go on to receive an award for four perfect years of design and drafting work. This of course, was his favorite subject.

Non school activities during the high school years were divided between a job at a local TV station as the evening shift studio technician and playing stand-up bass with a Dixie Land band (the other five members were in their sixties and seventies; Shawn was sixteen). Just a few short years before this, Shawn had begun to teach himself how to play his father's upright bass. Richard showed Shawn the proper strumming technique, and had given him some pointers on the bass... the rest was left for Shawn to fumble through and learn on his own (of course with God's help through the gift of an ear for music). To this point, Shawn had only played the bass at home during family functions, or accompanying the family radio.

One afternoon, Richard read of a local restaurant that was having a band for the evening's entertainment. Both Shawn and Richard decided to go and enjoy the Dixie-Land music; one of the music genres that Shawn had enjoyed playing to. The duo arrived at the restaurant a little early, both to assure finding the restaurant and acquire good seats; all within a timely manner.

It wasn't too long after the band began playing, that both Richard and Shawn noticed that the group was missing one critical instrument... a bass (the bass player seemed to be missing also)! After the first set was finished, and the band took their first break, Richard got up from his seat and approached the band leader.

"Good evening. My name is Richard, and this is my son Shawn. We love what you guys are doing up here, but we are a little confused... do you guys not have a bass player?"

The leader, somewhat embarrassed by the moment, stated "Yes, we actually do have a bass player. But we honestly don't know where he is!"

Much to Richard's surprise, Shawn spoke up and said "Well, we actually live just ten minutes down the road; I could go home and grab my bass if you'd like me to sit in with you."

Richard could instantly see the thoughts running through the band leader's mind. His facial expression indicated that "Thanks, but no thanks on a young kid with an electric bass playing rock music" was going to be his reply. Quickly (and correctly) assessing the looming band leader's response, Richard spoke up with "No, no! He (Shawn) actually plays an upright bass, he has been playing for years, and he probably knows most of the tunes you are playing."

Somewhat taken back by Richard's statement, the band leader replied "Well then sure! Let's give it a shot!" Within a short period of time, Shawn returned with bass in hand. Without any time to rehearse, he was on stage playing bass to "Hello Dolly", "When the Saints go marching in", and a bevy of other Dixie-land standards. This marked the beginning of Shawn being involved professionally with a variety of bands over the coming years.

Aviation wise, Shawn began rebuilding a single place, *Fisher-101*—a home-built aircraft of forty horsepower resembling an *Aeronca Champ*. The craft had been damaged during a landing by its former owner, which afforded Shawn the opportunity to buy the craft for one thousand dollars. He, his Dad, and a neighbor, Bill Blohm, traveled to Long Island New York to get the yellow bird.

With much shifting of furniture, twisting and turning of airplane parts, and ultimately the temporary removal of the staircase, the craft was positioned in the house basement. As a complete rehab of the *Fisher* was started, Shawn informed his Dad that a completely welded fuselage and tail assembly were being given to him by a father and son who were active flyers and friends at the local airport. Shawn had been friends with the father and son team for a couple years, and had even helped them construct and maintain their RV-6 homebuilt aircraft. The gift was completely unexpected. Could this be?

Sure enough, within a week, Shawn and Richard were following directions to a remote farm in the hills of western Connecticut. There at the destination were the father and son aviators and the *Mong Sport* Bi-Plane project that was promised to Shawn. While Shawn and the son were loading the craft onto a trailer, Dad Theiss was both pleased and humbled to hear the father state, "You must be very proud of Shawn. He certainly knows what he wants to do in life, and we know that he will appreciate our gift to him."

The trip back home with a second aircraft in tow was almost surreal; not much was spoken, but smiles were abundant for the whole trip. Once again, the "dance of the furniture" took place to allow the Mong Sport to join the Fisher in the basement. Now their house basement was completely filled with some fifteen model airplanes of various sizes and stages of completion and the parts of two full sized aircraft.

Yes, the innate love and understanding of "flying things" was quite obvious in Shawn to everyone around him. However, the key as to what direction in aviation he would take was actually indicated when he shocked the indoor model airplane builders of the New England states by successfully flying a McDonald's plastic hamburger box. Not only did the rubber band, prop-driven box fly, but it did so extremely well. The family's mountain side neighbor, Bill Blohm, suggested that the idea be presented to McDonald's, along with the offer to supply the propeller, rubber band, and the few other parts necessary to complete the learning and fun project. Dad Theiss did a sheet of drawings and wrote an explanation that was sent to the corporate offices of the fast food chain.

Within a few weeks, a letter was received stating that despite their great interest in the idea, the restaurant chain would not be able to pursue it as the current plastic burger boxes were being replaced with cardboard boxes. It seemed that the government was condemning the use of plastic food boxes, and McDonalds was conforming as quickly as possible. In retrospect, the firm of Ronald the Clown, as it turned out, was the only fast food provider to cave to the government pressure.

Nevertheless, cardboard would never fly as well as the much lighter foam plastic, and the turn down was a great disappointment. Almost forgotten, the success with flying a hamburger box would, in future years, prove to be one of the greatest blessings in Shawn's aviation career. God indeed knows the future.

To this point in Shawn's life, as one might expect, his home life, Christian raising, basic interests, God-given talents, along with now seventeen very active years on planet earth, all played a part in the molding of a driven youth who's future was a given—a life steeped in aviation. In fact, his love for aviation even led him to acting in a full length video movie titled "Welcome to Your Past and Present." The video production by RBY studios of Connecticut told the story of a young boy's fascination with flying things and followed his life from the first encounter with a real aircraft (*Waco Cabin Bi-plane*) to his first solo flight in a *Cub*.

Though well done, Shawn never made the attempt to do any acting, on stage or in front of the camera, again.

Back in the '30s...
Candlelight Farms Airport, near Candlewood Lake in New Milford, was the scene of "Welcome to your past and present," a video movie about a young boy growing up with an interest in aviation, by Flying Video Productions, a subsidiary of RBY Recording and Video of Southbury. Left to right are Moria Jones, soundperson, Evan Jones, cameraperson, Jack Jones, producer, and Richard Theiss, director. Roger Dunham of New Milford pilots his 1937 Waco plane. The movie will be released on videocassette in late November.

Shawn acted in and flew for scenes in "Welcome to Your Past and Present."

WORLD WIDE INFLUENCE

It would seem appropriate to consider the influence of international activities on Shawn's life at this time. Although only a high school senior, the fall-out effect of the taking down of the famed Berlin Wall would again call for the pending move of the Theiss family.

The resulting ease of tension between the United States and Russia brought about the cancellation of US Military contracts. Many of the contracted firms were located in the northeast section of the country. Richard had left Warner Brothers some time earlier, and was now engineering in fields directly related to these military industries. He soon found himself needing another source of income. However, none was to be found in Connecticut. In fact, the entire state was such that every other home was up for sale. Personal and business bankruptcies were at an all time high. Eventually, the Theiss mountain side home joined the listings of availability. Where to go now?

Ever wise in times such as this, Shawn's mother suggested that Dad Theiss consider the return to Salem, Ohio—his place of birth and childhood. As she recalled, almost every family trip taken from both Florida and Connecticut ended up in Richard's beloved Salem, Ohio. She reasoned too that now some sixty years old, her husband should at least enjoy any future work amid familiar surroundings. These thoughts were true blessings of the Lord. Why not? She always prayed about such concerns.

As point man for the next move, Richard (while living with an older sister, Marian Whipkey) returned to the E.W. Bliss Company engineering department. This was, in fact, a return to the firm he first joined while attending Kent State University some forty years earlier.

A few months later, Shawn graduated from high school. Originally, Shawn had thoughts of moving back to his state of birth and possibly going onboard with Walt Disney in Florida just as his father had years ago. But with the current circumstances and the inevitable move of his parents to Ohio, Shawn found himself torn. The original plan sounded fun and exciting, but the news coming back from Ohio indicated there could be a very promising future there.

After much prayer and consideration, Shawn joined his father in Ohio, and came to enjoy some of the same occupations enjoyed by the elder Theiss many years before. By this time, during the bedtime conversations with Dad, Shawn had heard all about Salem, Ohio and its streets, alleys, and places of business and recreation. In Shawn's mind, this was really home.

Overnight it seemed Shawn was immersed in the activities of his new home—work, new friends, girls, church activities, and visits to all of the local airfields. But after a temporary break, it became evident that Shawn should pursue his college degree. If not pursued soon, the brief hiatus could easily become a permanent state of being.

In the United States, at that time, there were only two aviation schools of importance, at least in Shawn's mind. Embry Riddle was located in Florida, some twelve hundred miles to the south. The other consideration, Beaver College School of Aviation, was located just across the Pennsylvania state line (twenty two miles at best). Wow! Mom's cooking, home at night, and aviation school too! How good could it be?

It all sounded great, other than Mom Theiss would be still babysitting the Connecticut home site in hopes that someday it might sell. Although the asking price had been drastically cut, to date, only one doctor from Long Island had looked at the property. His wife, being a horse lover, could find no place for grazing (other than the mountain side parking lot located to the front of the house) Good-bye to the chance to sell. The other interest was a movie studio wanting to lease it to film a movie.

When the realtor offered to take care of the property until it sold, plans were made to pack up and head for Ohio. The move included a truckload of two of Shawn's three, full-sized aircraft, along with numerous models, engines, etc. The fuselage of Shawn's double winged project (started back at the first Connecticut home, but damaged on the move to this home) would have to be left behind; the moving van was full to the brim.

With the final move of Hope and the household items coming about quickly, there was no time to formally search for a house to purchase. However, a good sized, three story home became available for rent at the perfect time and for the perfect price. This home would more than meet the immediate needs of the Theiss Family while affording the time to recoup some of the finances expended on the east coast.

On former visits to the Salem area, Shawn had developed a friendship with a Mr. Kenny Koons, owner of Koons Airfield located just west of the Salem city limits. This, of course, would be the new home for Shawn's *Fisher 101*.

The older pilot and instructor received the craft with mixed concern. It was, after all, of the home-built category. Kenneth Koons was a purest, to say the least, when it came to aircraft. People had no need to build their own aircraft. That is what airplane manufacturers were for. That was that.

As with many things in Shawn's life, he had an inside track when it came to the attitude of the airfield owner—music. Kenney Koons was an enthusiastic player of home styled country music. The guitar and accordion were his choice of instruments, and, oh yes, he sang and yodeled, of sorts.

Many were the evenings spent with Kenney on the accordion, Kenney's son, Dave, on the guitar, and Shawn on the bass. These sessions were located around the heater in the small office area of Koons field. Shawn's homebuilt plane had a hangar roof over it—no small price to have been paid.

Richard with Shawn's Fisher 101 at Koon's Airfield.

As Shawn traveled east toward the Beaver College School of Aviation, he passed another airfield along the Ohio/Pennsylvania border. In time, he and Dad Theiss stopped by to investigate the newfound flying field.

Blessing on blessings! The owner of this flying field and factory complex was none other than Ernie Carlson, the producer of a fine line of homebuilt kits. Within a few visits, Shawn was scheduled to head back to Florida with the Carlson Aviation team as a factory representative at Shawn's old stomping grounds, Sun N' Fun.

In the meantime, having reassembled his now finished *Fisher 101*, Shawn had been performing initial high-speed taxi runs with the craft preparing for the first flight. Shawn planned to get a few test flights in before the trip to the Sun N' Fun fly-in with Carlson.

The evening before leaving for Florida, Shawn and Richard (camera in hand) headed for Koons field. Before leaving the house, Mom Theiss reminded them both to be home by six o'clock. She would have cooked dinner and expected them to enjoy it while it was still hot.

Having agreed to the terms of the dinner schedule, the two looked forward to an early evening of test flights. In less than an hour, the Fisher was ready to again reach for the blue sky above. This time though, Shawn fully intended to fly. It was decided that Shawn would make a few lift offs before flying the pattern. As expected, all seemed well with the craft and its response to the controls. Before closing the cabin door, Dad Theiss reminded Shawn that one time around the pattern would have to be it for now. It was almost six—dinner time.

With Dad's camera clicking away, Shawn taxied down the runway, turned the craft around, opened the throttle, and into the air he went. Within a few moments, the seemingly normal take off had turned into a possible panic situation. Something had suddenly happened to the plane's power source; it wasn't developing the needed thrust required to climb over the obstructions at the east end of the field. The engine was running properly, but the craft simply was not climbing as it should. Compounding the now serious situation, Shawn had passed the point of no return. Time for a split second decision.

Quickly assessing the situation, Shawn realized that at his current rate of climb, it would be nearly impossible to clear the telephone lines along the roadway at the east end of the runway. And even if he could clear the phone lines, there was a line of trees about two hundred feet beyond the phone lines that stood some seventy feet tall. To top it all off, there were trees to either side of the runway that would prevent his making any avoidance turns.

His first thought was to build air speed by holding the nose down and flying under the wires. With enough speed, Shawn was sure he could make it up and over the tree line, therefore providing another chance to find something suitable for a forced landing beyond them.

Committing to the idea, Shawn lowered the nose of the craft to fly under the wires. Just then, two passing cars and a box truck slowed to a near stop to watch the approaching plane. So much for the plugged up space beneath the low hanging wires! Now he would have to attempt to fly over the wires with a sick power plant.

Witness to the pending disaster was Richard, camera still at the ready, but recording none of the past some twenty seconds activity. His early response was to call upon the one who could provide all that would be needed to bring the younger Theiss through the present situation. He prayed God's protection as he watched the yellow and blue craft miss snagging the wires by mere inches.

Some five miles to the east in Salem, at home, Hope Theiss finished setting the dinner table and looked at the clock above the sink. Six minutes till six. "They'll be late again," she thought. And then, she felt a chill and the need to pray for Shawn. Without hesitation she moved to the dining room, went to her knees, and prayed for God's protection of her test pilot son. She had always prayed when one of her men was in the air, but somehow, this was different.

Had she been on site, she would have seen Shawn fighting desperately for enough altitude to clear the wires, then the tall trees now only some fifty feet to his front. Instead, it was Richard who froze as he watched the plane almost completely clear the tallest branches, but then the left wingtip snagged onto a single, sturdy, top branch.

The branch held tightly to the inner structure of the fabric covered wood craft. Shawn still had enough air speed to pivot rotate 180 degrees, then hitting the mass of the trees branches that would ultimately send he and the plane crashing straight down through the many limbs below.

By this time, Richard had reached his parked car. Automatically he opened the door as he watched the aircraft chopping and smashing its way to the ground. The sound of wood on wood was sickening, as was the ground shaking thud that indicated the end of the horrendous situation. But at what cost?

The Theiss's white, Ford Thunderbird practically flew in the direction of the crash. Now weaving through the stand still traffic, Dad turned the car and jumped the ditch between the roadway and the crash site.

As happens many times when God works his magic, Richard could not believe his eyes. The final impact had burst the front of the cabin completely open. Through it emerged the young test pilot—face glowing from the realization of what had just transpired.

Shawn with his ex-Fisher 101 next to Koon's Airfield.

"Praise God! Dad, I'm all right!" Later, examination revealed two small quarter-inch-long cuts—one on his right cheek, the other on his left knee. And that was it. The scenarios are endless of what injuries could have been sustained, not to mention death.

God's protective presence was in evidence as a mother was picking wild flowers with her six-year-old daughter just a short distance from where Shawn had crashed. She was indeed a firsthand witness. Her response was also an answer to prayer. She, a former flight attendant and nurse, having quickly assessed Shawn's condition, called for her husband to load and remove the aircraft parts on his flat bed trailer. "Where do you want us to take it?" she asked Shawn. Having dealt with the FAA previously, she knew it could end up being a messy situation if a report had to be filed and an investigation performed.

"Home!" he said. His mom would be waiting there. Shawn and Richard followed close behind.

As the truck and trailer were leaving, the State Highway patrol pulled up. However, the officer never got out of the car, and Richard and Shawn didn't stop. Whatever their interest, the Theiss family never heard a word from them. Another blessing!

Through the traffic lights and stop signs of Salem, Shawn and Richard become separated from the truck and trailer. It was an anxious moment for Hope as she watched the truck and trailer pull into the driveway. The truck she did not recognize; the contents of the trailer, she did.

As the cold chill of realization ran through her body, a young woman jumped from the vehicle to quickly announce, "He's okay! Shawn is alright!"

In time, it was established that Hope had prayed at the precise moment when Shawn crashed through the stand of trees. Coincidence? Not so! For the believer, in times of concern, you pray. The outcome from that point is in God's hands. Whatever the answer to that prayer, you accept. In this case, Shawn was safe and sound. Great was the praise in the Theiss household that evening.

Within twenty-four hours of his harrowing test flight, Shawn was on his way to Florida with the Carlson Aircraft team. The point of destination was Lakeland and the Sun N' Fun EAA fly-in. Inside, Shawn wondered how the recent traumatic experience would affect his love of aviation. He had heard tale of pilots so traumatized from similar experiences that they could no longer bring themselves to crawl back into a plane, let alone fly again.

The next week would be spent among the people and planes that made up the young pilot's dream world, and the eighteen year old would be required to be enthusiastic and confident and to fly demonstrations. As he crawled into the Carlson cockpit and began to buckle in for the first flight demonstration of the show, a cold chill ran through him. He closed his eyes. *I will not let this stop me*, he thought. He took a deep breath, turned the ignition switch to on, yelled, "Clear," and pushed the ignition switch. As the engine rumbled to life, the cold chill quickly dissipated. He was where he needed to be again—where he wanted to be again.

Florida at this time of year was relatively calm, weather wise, and provided a fantastic week for flying and healing. However, less than six months later, hurricane Andrew would hit Florida with a punch that left the community flattened, both emotionally and physically (for the most part). Little did anyone know this was the proverbial calm before the storm.

LAYING THE FOUNDATION FOR A NEW DIRECTION

Three days after the storm had passed, Richard received a call from Robert MacDonald, an engineer friend of the family who had enjoyed numerous partnerships with both Richard and Hope, all having to do with flying and design engineering. This call would be a request for Richard's temporary return to Florida. It was hoped that he would join MacDonald in the re-design and reconstruction of a large block of demolished homes. In time, it was agreed that a month or so could be devoted to that end.

Early in the absence of his father, Shawn became aware of the plight of another former friend of the family, air show personality, Bob Hoover, who was a top former Air Force jet jockey. For the past some years, Bob had been thrilling air show audiences with his power-off aerobatics in a twin-engine Shrike Commander. More recently however, he had been grounded by a disgruntled FAA official for a minor health infraction. The ruling was upheld even after the health issue had been corrected. "Good grief," mused Shawn. "If this could happen to a guy like Bob Hoover, it could happen to Dad!" (He had to be nearly as old.) As Shawn pondered the problem, one thing became evident—the only recourse left for older pilots was to fly ultralights. However, this could not sit well with his Dad and maybe a lot of others too.

To that point, most ultralights were open tube and cloth structures with seats that resembled lawn chairs. Nope. Shawn's Dad would never stand for looking at the earth below from between his legs. His better judgment knew that old-time pilots wanted to at least feel that they were sitting in something, not on it. Armed with years of intimate association with flying things, his aviation studies, and a direct channel to the greatest designer to ever exist (God), he set out to solve the problem.

A single seat craft of very light materials, properly designed, certainly seemed possible. And, what was to prevent it from having the appearance of a standard aircraft you could sit in? Then too, standard stick and rudder controls would also do well with the old timers. Hey! How about an open cockpit bi-wing? Yea! This could be interesting!

The only problem was FAA part 103, the section of the FAA bible that set out the parameters for an ultralight. Shawn's main concern at this point in time was the allowable weight for such a craft. It would be no easy task to include all that he determined to be necessary at a mere 254 pounds maximum.

An aircraft engineer had been working with a Dow Chemicals rigid foam board for certain parts of home-built aircraft. It surely was a light enough material, but then, how strong was the stuff? Some tests would have to be run after framing the Styrofoam with sections of Sitka Spruce aircraft wood. Now another real concern came to mind—Aircraft Spruce was becoming very expensive. In fact, money, or rather the lack of it, could mess up the entire project.

That pending problem was put aside as Shawn went to his drawing board. With prayer, the needed money would be in the hands of the Miracle Worker. Shawn would simply trust God.

Over the next month, Shawn's off-the-drawing-board activities centered around girls (Zoe and Rhonda) and a fast motor bike. The latter was the scourge of his parents. No matter what his argument might be in favor of the two wheeled transportation, Mom and Dad were hard pressed to understand his desire to flirt with pending disaster.

During a near heated discussion on the subject, Shawn stated, "My friends think you both are weird. It doesn't seem to bother you when I test fly an airplane, but let me go bike riding with them, and it's like the end of the world!" Throughout the next many years, the facts of the subject remained unchanged. Day or night, when Shawn went riding, there was no rest for his parents.

When Richard flew into Pittsburgh, PA., Shawn and his mother were both happy to have him back from Florida. Shawn in particular seemed anxious to get Dad home for a waiting surprise. The fact that his father had just spent a long days' travel because of a lightning strike on the US Air 737 in which he had flown, meant little to the budding air-craft designer. When finally home, Shawn hustled his elder to the third floor pad and the drawing board. There it was! Three views of a single seat, open cockpit, double winger with an in-line cowling and sleek wheel pants. For the world it looked like a golden thirties racing plane.

Shawn studied his Dads face. After all, this design was for him and all older pilots who might face the wrath of the FAA at some future time. The appreciative smile that crept over his father's face spoke volumes. "Hey! She's a beauty!" Dad burst. "What are you using for power?" He was hooked. Now Shawn started to reel him in. "With forty horses, it qualifies as an ultralight." That did it.

Tired or not, Dad listened to Shawn's plans to market the craft as a kit. The complete business plan was such that the elder Theiss wondered when his son had time for dating, eating, sleeping, or riding that confounded bike of his. Once again it seemed Shawn had made up his mind to go into the aircraft manufacturing business. Knowing his son, it was now just a matter of time until the smell of aircraft glue permeated the house.

He was right. The project started in the basement with side fuselage frames made of Dow blue foam board and long grain, white pine (white pine was discovered to have practically similar strength qualities as spruce, but for less money). At least it was a reasonable start (dollar wise).

As progress was being made, anyone could see that the size of this craft was such that it may well spend the rest of its life encased within the walls of the basement. That is, unless something was done to the cellar stairs and side door entrance frame. It was. Removal of the stairs and part of the door frame provided for the fuselage to now rest in the first floor family room. When the tail group joined the fuselage and wing ribs were readied for final assembly, Hope put her foot down.

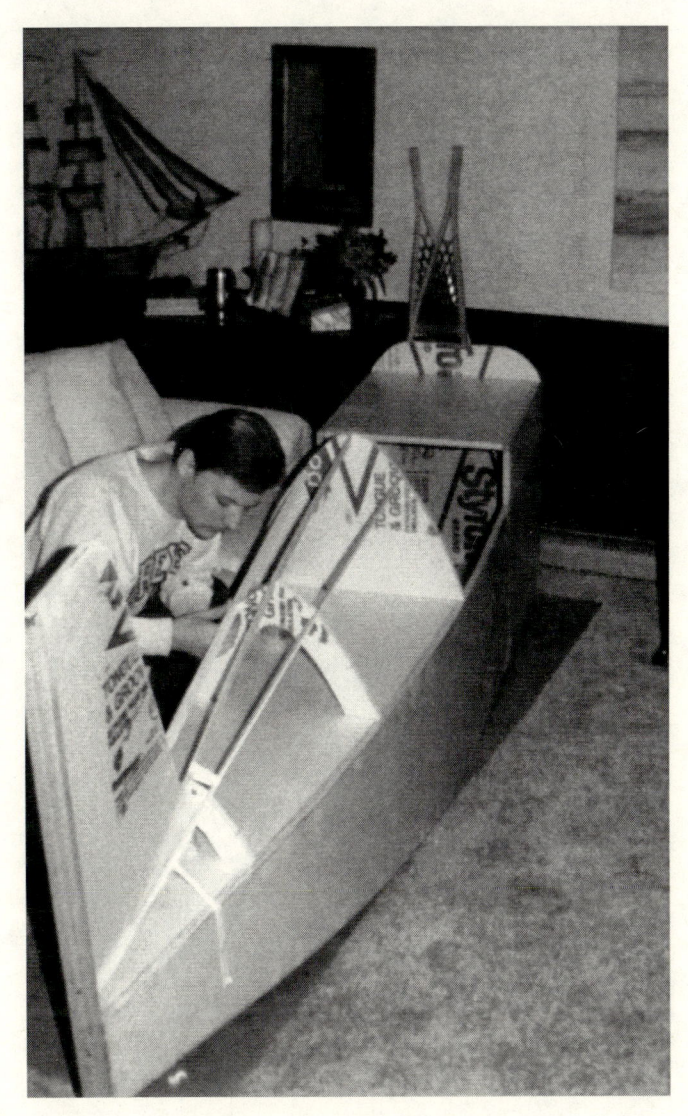

The new Speedster Fuselage in Mom's
family room…but not for long.

SURPRISE SURPRISE | 67

Shawn's new business or not, she could see her home fast becoming a hangar. She, being furniture savvy, had no plans for sitting in or on an airplane in her home. After a short search and contact with some local friends, a new home was found for the aspiring company. The parts were soon moved to a small building just north of Salem. For the next sixteen months, the location served as the proto-shop for the newly formed Theiss Aviation, Inc.

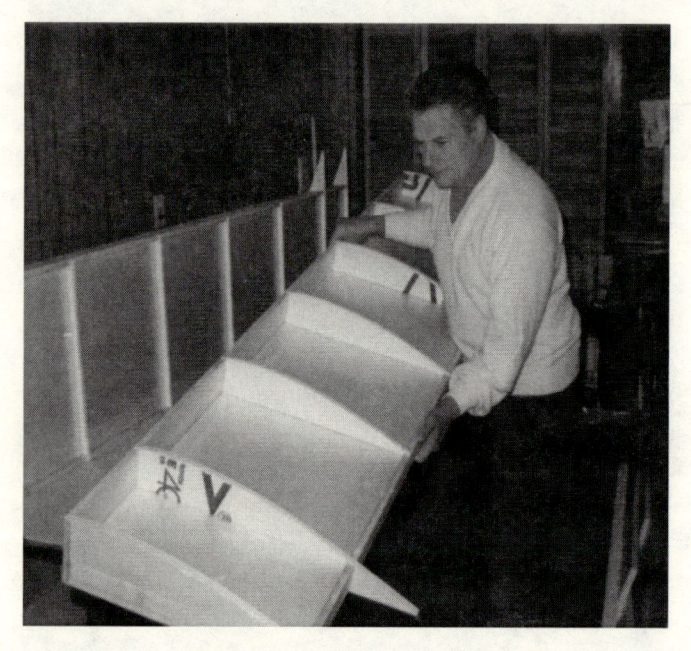

Wing panels in the basement.

Yes, Shawn had officially founded Theiss Aviation and staffed its officers with his father as vice president, and his mother, Hope, as secretary/treasurer. As president and chief executive officer, Shawn retained 50 percent of the total stock; the remaining shares to be split between the other two officers.

Profoundly established at the first official meeting was the action of prayer as an integral part of all decision making. Indeed, all future flights to be made by pilots of the firm would occur only after a prayer for safety and success was offered to the Heavenly Father. The involvement of God in every facet of the firm was to be undeniable.

The Speedster ready for its fabric covering.

The proto-type craft, which was to become known as the *Speedster*, was nearing completion when one Richard Beck (a former Taylor Craft and Piper engineer) became known to Shawn. Actually, Dick Beck had been the president of the Petrol Pups model airplane club that Dad Theiss had belonged to many years before. Beck was considered to be an answer to prayer when he offered to act as verification engineer on the *Speedster* project. Not being laden with money, the terms of the offer were music to Shawn's ears.

Around the same time, Shawn signed on to play upright bass with a professional bluegrass band in the local area called Get out and Push. It seemed the perfect way to help finance the company until the sale of kits could be realized.

Another source of money was presented by way of the Theiss' former Connecticut mountain-side neighbor, Bill Blohm. Bill and his wife Ruth had stopped by on a trip west and offered to buy a second craft that had been started.

When the *Speedster* had been assembled with its wings in place, Richard discovered that when seated in the cockpit his vision was impaired by the thickness of the top wing (the top wing was designed to sit on the top of the fuselage, and the pilot would look over the wing as opposed to under it). Although Shawn could easily see over the top wing, Richard was too short.

The second plane was started with the upper forward fuselage section re-designed to correct the vision problem for shorter pilots. In addition, the tail was slightly modified as was the top wing. The result was an attractive sport version of the *Speedster* to be named, the *Sportster*. Great! Now the flying public had a choice. The second craft moved toward completion with the Blohm shot in the arm (so to speak).

As the *Speedster* was moved from the prototype shop to a local airport (Salem airpark), Dick Beck issued a report on the strength (stress analysis) of the craft. His verbal statement was, "That baby is a little fort!" And so it proved to be!

Finished and ready to fly.

Winter moved in fast with a goodly amount of snow—enough to shut down the planned test flights for the winter months. However; a few pre-snow taxi tests had the airports A&E/A&P mechanic Bob Scott (who had been a former flight engineer with US Air.) hot to trot. He and a Texas trucking firm owner were constant visitors to the hangar and then, unexpectedly, showed up at the house with an offer to buy thirty kits of the *Speedster*! Their plan was to pre-build the craft into partially built kits such as almost finished fuselage, tail group, wings, etc. This of course would be re-sold at a higher price.

Although it sounded great, test flights were still to be made in the spring of that year. Shawn would be willing to talk after the first twenty hours of flight time had been completed. The future looked very good indeed. Winter snow storms had curtailed most flight activity at the Salem Air Park. For Theiss Aviation, it was a time for planning the many other concerns that would be required of a firm looking to a successful future. A shop of size would be needed as would workers to staff it. Then too, an air strip would be a must. Promotion and sales would require their share of time and effort. Good heavens, what could all of this cost?

As Hope feared, these two men officers of the firm would look to her for most of the needed funding. After all, she was the firm's Secretary/Treasurer.

Being skilled at stretching the dollar was something Hope found to be necessary of late. The job situation in Connecticut had drained family funds even before the move to Salem, Ohio. Now she was expected to perform magic as Theiss Aviation's president prodded forward.

One thing was for sure, having the two planes on display at the Experimental Aircraft Association events was paramount for the success of the fledgling company. Shawn and his vice president had gone to the EAA Oshkosh Fly-in the past summer and knew that there was nothing on the market to rival the flying products of Theiss Aviation. Now was the time to go public.

It was decided that the firm would be in attendance for the 1996 Sun N' Fun fly-in. This was an EAA sanctioned event that Shawn's parents had been an active part of while with the Florida based Walt Disney Company.

Promptly, a call was placed to the Sun N' Fun officials requesting the registration forms necessary for an aircraft manufacturer to display their products. With these forms in hand, the next urgent need was apparent... transportation!

An enclosed trailer large enough to handle two planes, display units, tools etc. along with a van large enough to pull it were the needs to be satisfied.

Hope waved her magic wand. Attached to it was a credit card.

Next, Shawn ordered a large (Theiss Blue) banner heralding the company statement, "Essence of the Past in Products of the Present." This banner was long enough to cover the entire length of the custom made trailer.

Once again, the Secretary waved her wand!

Blue and white company stationary was next in what was fast becoming a long list of needs. The treasurer waved her wand again and again and again.

Time for some help! Back to the stage.

Under her management company Diversified Talent, Hope promoted a musical combo called The Four Notes. Now Shawn and his VP were playing for dances, stage shows, private parties, political events, street fairs, weddings, etc., all in an effort to supply the necessary funding required to fulfill the needs of Theiss Aviation.

In addition, Shawn was performing with Get Out and Push on an ever increasing schedule. Music was now vying for Shawn's precious aviation time, but was indeed needed for the financing of his fledgling manufacturing firm. He played on.

As final arrangements were being made for the Florida air event business trip, Richard received a call from Dick Beck (their verification engineer) asking if he, Richard, might come on down for a little talk over the lunch hour. "Of course!" was Richard's response. "What's up?" he asked. "I'll explain when you get here." The ten or so mile trip to Beck's had Richard wondering as to the reason for the request.

"I was just wondering," Beck said, "if, when I die, it might be possible for you and Shawn to spread my ashes over cloud three?"

Still somewhat confused, Richard almost blurted, "We'd be happy to, but, why are we talking about this?"

"Just was wondering." He cut the subject off. Conversation then turned to old "remember when" stories and the status of the new Theiss aircraft.

One week later, Hope got a call from Nada, Dick Beck's wife. "Richard died this morning," she stated flatly. The unexpected news was shocking and heartbreaking.

Later, Nada revealed that Dick had been dying from cancer for some time, but didn't want Shawn to know about it for fear that it might distract from his test flying of the new designs. This love and concern of one airman for another was touching to say the least. All three officers of the Theiss firm were greatly saddened; a true friend and partner in aviation had been lost.

In Shawn's mind, Dick Beck had become family; even more. How many families have their own verification engineer? Well, had. Shawn had also wanted Dick to share in the success of the new designs; now, he would never know.

After the funeral Nada told Shawn that Dick wanted him to have all of his model planes, tools, and radio control equipment. When picking up the model plane items, Richard foolishly left the radio control equipment behind. After all, the father and son modeling team were free flight flyers. The model planes they flew had no such gear.

Barely a week went by when Hope received another unexpected and saddening call from the son of Dick and Nada. She too had just passed away. Life indeed was very fragile.

So too, seemed the house in which the Theiss family lived. As if the stress of preparing for the EAA event was not enough, compounded by the swift loss of their good friends, their rental property had been sold to make way for a Burger King fast food restaurant. Time again for house hunting.

At last, God opened the door once again to an old, stately Victorian house in need of a little TLC—a place large enough to take all of the furniture, and blessing upon blessing, a structure for a small shop on the same property. Actually, the very old structure (1845) had originally been a carriage house, then later an auto barn. Now it would be a plane barn.

As his parents worked to restore the century house, Shawn cleaned and set up the two storied barn with benches and tools. This was not going to be the best of work areas—hot in the summer, cold in the winter—but it was good enough for now. Shawn was a survivor.

Soon enough, the fifteen room house had the overflow of aircraft parts once again taking over. Not the large parts such as wings and fuselage but smaller parts such as tail units, landing gears, etc. Hope would have to contend with the situation later. For now, it was air show time at Sun N' Fun in Florida. Special bracketing had been built into the trailer and all hands were required to load the many items. The last minute rush could always be expected. It had been like that for model contests over the years, and would be the same for the coming air oriented events. You could call it a sort of tradition.

Look Out Aviation Buffs—Here We Come!

Just in time, the Theiss Aviation entourage hit the snow covered highways of the frigid north for the long awaited trip to Florida. As they moved southward it seemed they were being borne along by a mass of dirty, filthy cars, vans, and trucks. Boy would the car wash people of the south make out this spring.

All went well for the first part of the trip. If they could keep the pace, they could reach their destination by five or six in the evening. They happily hummed along with the music playing on the van radio.

With Hope and a granddaughter following the company van and trailer, Shawn often checked the rear view mirrors; however, it was the right side view that began to hold his attention. Something seemed to be dripping from the trailers right side access door. What could it be? All liquids were sealed and fastened down. Well, whatever it is, it would have to wait for a place to pull over. Within a mile, a road sign revealed a roadside rest area one mile ahead. Shawn heaved a sigh of relief.

But as they pulled into the rest area, his feeling of relief disappeared. As he moved around the rear of the trailer, he was smacked with the strong order of gasoline. The combustible fuel was now dripping from the rear loading door as well as the side access. Now, panic prevailed. It was taking too long to unlock and lower the rear ramp door, only to confirm a compact load of airplane parts, tools, and display items. Somewhere within that maze held the source of the problem.

As the trailer was being unloaded, Shawn and Richard exchanged determinations.

"Dad, it's the fuel tank!"

"Gotta be," Richard agreed.

"Maybe a fuel line," Shawn speculated.

"Road vibration could do it!"

In time the worst was realized. The fuel tank, located in the front of the *Speedster* fuselage, had split at a bottom edge. Only now was it remembered that in the hustle and bustle of packing everything, the tank had not been completely drained before the trip. This had become a case of too smart, too late.

Trying not to draw attention, Hope and granddaughter, Dawn, filled and carried jugs of drinking water from the nearest fountain to where the fuel lay under the rear of the trailer to dilute it as quickly as possible. It was working. No fire. No danger.

Even if it were only one gallon that had drained from the tank, it was enough to settle into the bottom of the fuselage. In a short amount of time it would eat away at the foam parts, leaving only the wood and painted fabric covering. To forestall this as much as possible, Shawn slit the fabric on the bottom of the fuselage and allowed the gas to flow out. For a few minutes, Shawn sat on the curb beside the trailer visibly distraught and silent. The *Speedster* was obviously damaged to the point of now being un-airworthy, and the *Sportster* was being taken for static display only as it was not finished yet. At this point, was there any use in continuing to the event? Daylight was burning and a direction had to be chosen.

The out and out joy in evidence before the stop had taken a turn to stone cold silence. It was a time for reflection, contemplation, and prayer. Some considerable time, effort, and money had gone into the trailer contents being towed to an event that could launch the tiny Theiss firm into the annals of great American aircraft companies—that is, if there were a product to be displayed and demonstrated. If ever Christian faith had a purpose to be realized, it would be now. Surely God had a reason for allowing this to have occurred, at this time and in this place. Given time, He would reveal it.

After a brief discussion mingled with blank stares and more moments of silence, it was decided to continue. The trailer was quickly repacked, and the Theiss Aviation team rolled back onto the highway.

Moments of weariness turned into hours. There was more than enough time to rehash the events that had led to this place and time; more than enough time to wonder what good could possibly come from this situation. And then, the entry gates of the Sun N' Fun event loomed ahead. "We're here! For what? Speak to us Lord!"

Old Aviation friends, from the time when the Theisses had coordinated Disney air-show activities at Sun N' Fun, were there to welcome the well-worn travelers.

Much had changed from the former Disney days, but none so much as Shawn himself. The little boy who had determined to design and build real airplanes was now a young man who, by all indications, had pulled it off. All were waiting to see what magic the new white trailer contained.

Fortunately, it was quickly turning dark and all would have to wait until the next day for the ramp door to be opened.

The evening was Florida warm. It was completely dark now, and most vendors in the area were attending the various parties provided by the various manufactures of aircraft supplies. Distant lights and laughter gave indication as to their locations.

No such frivolity was enjoyed by the Theiss team. In the dark of night, the rear ramp door of the trailer had been opened. Quietly, surrounding parts had been unloaded, and, the *Speedster* fuselage emerged in whatever condition it was presently in. The smell of fuel was again overwhelming.

A lone flashlight was used to survey the damage. In retrospect, being of Christian faith had its advantage with the hushed expressions of the crew as they realized the extent of the problems to be overcome. This was definitely a time for prayer.

Having placed the situation squarely in the hands of the Lord and with Shawn holding the tail of the fuselage off the lowered loading ramp, Richard proceeded to remove the damaged foam material from under the seat of the pilot. The effort left little else than wood stringers and fabric. The once unique and functional foam formers were now non-existent. Fortunately, the shape of that section of lower fuselage was flat and still intact.

Next, Shawn fashioned a flat of cardboard to cover the area that had been the cockpits flooring. Heaven forbid that anyone would attempt to sit in the plane over the next week. The fate of Theiss Aviation was now indeed in the hands of the heavenly Father… Would He, could He have mercy on anyone foolish enough to travel with gasoline in an aircraft fuel tank?

THE DAWN OF A NEW DAY

The rest of the first night at Sun N' Fun was much too short. Even though the general public would not be around for the set up of the display area, other firms would be handy to assess the new Theiss products. And so, the assembly of both aircraft and the elements of display were done in haste. Pretending that all was well, Shawn, Richard, and Hope were greatly relieved with the remarks of those who seemed duly impressed with the Theiss Aviation display area.

The morning after (the hectic night of reassembly at Sun 'n Fun, Florida).

By day's end, the Florida sun and atmosphere had pretty much done away with the odor of gasoline from around the Speedster. Somewhat relieved from the stress of the trip, the Theiss team slept much better their second night in Florida.

The next five days at Sun N' Fun proved most interesting. There were constant crowds of the interested, with cameras in hand and questions ever flowing. Then too, there were the magazine editors, writers, and camera persons all wanting this pose and that. Oh yes! Fear was realized when a featured article would require Shawn taxiing the *Speedster* for the cameras. Thank goodness the plane had not flown the required twenty hours necessary to fly at the event. Undoubtedly, the damaged fuselage would not have taken the stress of flight.

As Shawn taxied around the sod field, neither he nor the plane showed any signs of the former mishap. Unnoticed by the magazine reps were Shawn's broad shoulders being used to keep his full weight off of the damaged seat brace—something that required a lot of constant strength. But you could not see it in his face, and the magazines got the shots they were looking for.

All in all, the week at Sun N' Fun went surprisingly well. As hoped for, the acceptance of both Theiss craft was most favorable. The idea of an ultralight with the appearance of a standard aircraft struck a nerve with flying folk, especially those over fifty years of age. Shawn was correct in his assumptions made years before; older pilots just loved strut and wire braced airplanes.

The price set for the craft also sat well with potential buyers—$4995.95 did seem a bit low to those in the industry. How could Theiss make a good profit at that price? The Christian attitude behind all aspects of the business, including price fixing, was to give the best product for the most reasonable cost to the customer.

With the indication of much business ahead, it was also evident that much work was still to be done. A new fuselage would have to be built for the *Speedster*. The *Sportster* would have to be finished as well. A full set of drawings and the construction manual would demand considerable time. All foam parts would have to be hot-wired to shape (the procedure called for templates to be laid out and cut for each foam component in the airframe). Of course, a large cardboard shipping box needed to be designed for each craft. Everything in the kit was to be shaped and sized for easy assembly.

All things considered, the most important tool in the kit was masking tape. The entire plane was held together with masking tape while the glue dried. No nails or screws were used in the framing process.

At this time, it was determined by Shawn that Theiss Aviation would share the blessings they were enjoying as a new, small firm, by placing a New Testament Bible in each kit. That decision, in the minds of the other officers, only confirmed that God had indeed placed the right Theiss to serve as president and CEO.

Shortly after their return to the big, old house at 1100 Franklin Avenue in Salem, Ohio, life for the Theiss team became extra hectic. All of the functions mentioned before were now in full swing! As many as eighteen worldwide aviation magazines were hitting the book stores and stands, and the results were profound. Letters of interest and inquiry were arriving daily from the far corners of the earth. Many asked for a newsletter that had been offered at Sun N' Fun. Richard had assumed the editorship of such and found the available hours during the day growing increasingly scarce.

Even the normal hours of sleep were fast becoming a thing of the past. For those who had just obtained their copy of Flying Magazine and read about the new Theiss flying products, the fact that they were in China or Japan meant little when they picked up the phone to gain further information. On the receiving end of those calls were the bed-ridden who were expected to respond as if it were not 2:30 a.m. Dear Lord, what next?

Both floors of the barn were filled with airplanes and pre-built parts. The house basement was filled with wings while the kitchen dining area played host to tail sections. And to top it all off, the re-assembled *Speedster* (with new fuselage) was being tested by Shawn during the summer months.

In the midst of all that was being accomplished, it was decided that Shawn and Richard would need to attend the 1996 EAA Oshkosh Summer Fly-in. This, of course, would hopefully give some indication of any other firm running with the ideas Theiss displayed at Sun N' Fun a few months before.

The last minute decision had a drawback; only a two day weekend visit would be possible, and surely there would be no accommodations available. Not to be daunted, Shawn soon located a friend with a tent— not the usual pup tent they expected, but a new design which supposedly gave more head room; at least, the pictures on the box indicated it to be so.

They arrived at the Oshkosh EAA Campsite late Friday evening. With the sun quickly setting, there would be little time in which to erect their abode. As luck would have it, someone in the camp remembered seeing the two at Sun N' Fun. "Hey! Aren't you the guys that build those neat little ultralights?" The recognition, however appreciated, could not have come at a worse time.

Each of the several attempts at the assembly of the tent had the same conclusion—a slow collapse to a heap of braces and canvas; certainly nothing that resembled the picture on the box.

As a small crowd gathered to ask questions about the Theiss flying products, they were being treated to quite a show. Then, to make matters even worse, a dear, sweet little old lady (most probably in her late eighties) appeared and asked "May I be of some help? We have a tent just like it."

In what seemed to be a very short amount of time, she (with the flailing of her hands) made the confounded thing look just like its picture on the box!

Only the falling shadows of evening could have hidden the embarrassment written on the faces of Shawn and Richard, for they knew only too well the thoughts of those smirky-faced ones standing round about the tent site. "These guys design and build airplanes?" Oh, the humbling of God!

The Theiss team tent at the Summer, Oshkosh E.A.A. event. (A humbling experience.)

The upside to the venture was the realization that Theiss (for the time being) had the market cornered with the *Speedster* and *Sportster* designs. During their drive back to the Salem area, it was determined that all efforts would be targeted for the return to the 1997 Sun N' Fun event. By the fall of 1996, the company still had not accepted monies for orders; it simply was not ready to satisfy any orders.

In the meantime, the payments for home, cars, van, and trailer had to be met. In addition, there were the utilities, food, and gas to pay for. Shawn's college education hadn't come cheap. However, they had all been blessed with health and opportunities for employment.

Within a short time, the president and vice president were both working with the engineering department at the electric furnace company, a firm that designed and produced industrial furnaces for the steel industry. The secretary was engaged in full time home nursing—this while managing on stage musical performances for all three Theiss Aviation officers. Busy? Oh yes! Night and day.

Busy as they were, there was always time for the writing and producing of Church related programming. The First Friends Church of Salem provided for the use of the family's former Disney production experience. The Christmas and Easter seasons were most precious for all concerned.

LET IT SNOW! LET IT SNOW! LET IT SNOW!

Northeastern Ohio has always been known for its radically changing weather. A common expression is, "If you don't like the weather, wait a few minutes!" October of 1996 was a shining example. A pre-Halloween snow fall caught most folks by surprise, the Theiss firm included. Shawn had been having cooling problems with the Speedster's Kawasaki 440-A engine and needed as much good flying weather as possible to get the issue resolved. The Speedster's sleek, slim, in-line cowling gave the appearance of a golden age racer. It had been baffled and vented much the same as the racers. But being a 2-cycle engine, she still ran hot. At this rate, would Shawn be able to fly the required twenty hours before Sun N' Fun 1997? There was so much to be done, and so short was the time available. Could it be that at age twenty-four, Shawn had a lot on his plate? There was a still budding aviation business, a full-time engineering job, playing bass and singing with a blue grass band, playing bass with the Four Notes stage band, playing drums with the church praise band, oh, and yes, even time for a new girlfriend.

The social craze of the day was country line dancing. Everybody was doing it—young, old, rich, poor! Night clubs and dance clubs were promoting it as exclusive entertainment, and certain weeknights were dedicated solely to it. Dressed in attractive cowgirl attire, Charlene Crow caught the eye of Shawn during one of his get-away-from-it-all, leisure nights out. Eventually, Charlene was to occupy most of Shawn's leisure time.

Thus loaded down, Shawn continued on. The winter snows came, Thanksgiving came, and heavier winter snows continued. Christmas came with ample snow for Santa's sleigh, but it was much too much for Shawn's landing gears. His badly needed flight tests were non-existent.

Plans were being made for the firm's return to, Sun N' Fun 1997. The required retainers were sent off to the land of sunshine while Ohio was still being held in the grip of an extra nasty winter. Of course, time off for the aviation event had been pre-arranged with the Electric Furnace Company for both Shawn and Richard. This would be counted as their vacation time.

Too soon, it seemed, the trailer was again packed for the trip to Lakeland, Florida. This time, there would be no damaged fuel tank, no dripping gas, and no last minute repairs by the dark of night. The Theiss Aviation crew had grown by one. Charlene was on her way to the sunshine state for the first time as a member of the Theiss Team. The one thing that had not changed was the fact that, once again, Shawn had not been able to fly the required twenty hours for clearance to demonstrate the plane's flight characteristics. Much to Shawn's dismay, static displays would have to suffice again.

If anything, the second participation at the huge EAA event would prove to be most frustrating. The overwhelming attention and interest shown by the program attendees only compounded the fact that the firm was still not up to speed (kit production wise) as before, and the aviation magazines were all over Shawn and his creations. The editor of *Sport Pilot & Ultralights* asked that a bio be sent to their California office as they would be doing a feature article. If only Theiss Aviation were ready to roll. To this point, Shawn had only been able to perform short flights with the *Speedster*; enough to prove airworthiness of the design, but not enough to make Shawn comfortable in opening the flood gates to sell.

The long return trip to Ohio was spent mentally listing the most immediate needs of the company—the continued production of airplane parts, the design and development of packaging the kit (no small chore), the completion of the drawings and construction manual, of course, and, oh yes, solving the nagging problem of engine overheating to complete the flight testing regiment for the *Speedster*.

LOCATION, LOCATION, LOCATION

Woven into the pattern of company needs was the thread of physical location. For some months, the family had been looking for a small field suitable for building and testing of their aircraft. Their search took them to hill top strips and narrow valley flats. A few had buildings of various shapes and sizes. A small field at which Richard had flown when he was Shawn's age was available. Whitley Airport provided some great memories, but the asking price was a bit too much.

While the search went on, the *Speedster* had been moved from the Salem Air Park to Miller Field. The North Benton, Ohio, location was much better suited for the upcoming flight tests, and it was owned by a former school mate of Richard. Dick Gano and Richard had both learned to fly as students of Russ Miller many years before.

Over the next few weeks, Shawn conducted taxi and short flight tests at the new location. Although Miller Field had a hard surfaced runway some twenty six hundred feet long, the grass strip next to the hard top was used for all of the Theiss testing. Videos of all tests were being handled by Charlene. She, as it turned out, had the unique ability to remain completely focused on the craft, no matter what its attitude or condition of contact with the ground. Richard, on the other hand, though having considerable experience with video, was too concerned with the test pilot to remain calm during the unexpected, as was soon to be demonstrated.

The evening air was perfect for testing. Charlene was not available for filming that evening, so Shawn would fly, and Richard would video. When the taped flight was later reviewed, both Shawn and the *Speedster* were perfectly centered on the video screen during the take-off run and rotation. "Wow," thought Richard to himself, "this will be great promotional footage!"

As the bi-plane steadily climbed to two hundred feet, it remained perfectly centered in the viewer. The craft was flying very well, and the whole scene was picture perfect. Inside the *Speedster*, Shawn was using very little effort to fly the craft. She was steady and responsive to any little control input Shawn chose to administer. Shawn looked off the left wingtips to see the main hangar slowly pass below, then the west end of the runway; committed to flight at this point, all seemed to be going very well.

Then, suddenly, for no apparent reason to Richard, Shawn banked the craft sharply to the right and soon disappeared behind a stand of tall pine trees at the west end of the runway. In the cockpit, Shawn had turned his attention back to the dash panel to scan the instruments. Within seconds the feeling of situational wellness was replaced with contradicting fact; the engine cylinder head temperatures were well over the redline, and still climbing. Almost instantly, the engine RPMs began to decrease indicating that an engine seizure was fast approaching. Quickly assessing the situation, including location, altitude, and engine status, Shawn realized the inevitable—this plane was coming down, and there was nothing he could do to stop it from happening!

With all visual contact lost, Richard strained to hear the planes progress. He could hear enough to know that the engine had wound down to a complete stop. The next expected sound never came. Where was the sound of impact?

Shawn and the tiny *Speedster* had only achieved a couple hundred feet in altitude before the current situation began; not much time to prepare for much of anything, let alone a forced landing. However, Shawn knew that the field he was about to meet was not a smooth, hard surface like the runway he had cleared just seconds ago. Just a short time ago, while at the 1996 Sun N' Fun event, the Theisses (and the aviation community as a whole) lost another friend and old air show colleague. Charlie Hillard was killed when his *Hawker Sea Fury* (a low wing, WWII aircraft) experienced brake problems after landing in a crosswind, and flipped over on the ground. The tragedy was that it was not the impact of the flip that killed him; it was not being able to breathe from having his head pinned against his chest in the inverted craft. He suffocated before rescuers could reach him.

Flash forward—Shawn was in a craft where his head was almost the highest thing on top of the airframe, second only to the vertical fin and rudder. Despite having limited time to think things through, he knew that the small wheels on the *Speedster* would not roll far, if at all, in the undeveloped field below. This could very easily lead to the same demise as Charlie. "Dear God, what a terrible way to go!" Shawn quickly formed a plan; with the plane now flying dead stick, he would push the nose over to pick up a little speed, then within a few feet of touchdown, pull full back on the stick and try to stall the craft a few feet off the ground—a sparrow landing!

Back at Miller Field, the next some minutes were recorded by the now dangling camcorder. As the lens showed Richard's running feet, his voice could be heard, "Oh dear God! Please save our Shawn!"

At some point, the run led to the same car used to jump a ditch when Shawn had crashed through the trees at Koons Airport a few years before.

By instinct, Richard followed Shawn's flight path with the speeding car. At the end of the runway he turned right into a field of full grown soy beans. At a distance he could see the small white plane, sitting upright, and Shawn standing next to it. A cold chill shot through him. Was this a dream? Had God once again saved Shawn from disaster? Inspecting the landing site, indications were that the landing roll-out distance was very short. Shawn's quick laid plan, along with the mature soy bean growth (which had acted somewhat the same as arresting wires on an aircraft carrier's deck) had allowed the plane to land without disaster.

That nasty ole heating problem had caused the engine to completely seize. Shawn's plane was dead stick throughout most of his landing procedure. He was as calm as the current wind condition. After all, this was just another day in the life of a test pilot. It was becoming evident that Shawn had been blessed with yet another uncanny ability. When asked years later about his experiences in flight testing, Shawn was able to say that he remembered everything about each forced ("crash") landing, and that he never experienced fear or panic through any of them. God had truly blessed the young pilot with clear, focused, and calm thought process in times of crisis. This gift would be tested repeatedly in the years to come, both in and out of aircraft.

Sitting in the open trunk of the car, the downed pilot towed this somewhat damaged *Speedster* back to the hangar. Those darned soy beans could really do a number on the under carriage of a plane. But given the possible outcomes of the unwanted forced landing, both Shawn and Richard realized that a bent wheel axle and strained bungee strut were minor damage in comparison.

By the time the rework of the landing gear had taken place, the correction of the heating problem had also been accomplished by replacing the air-cooled engine, with a liquid cooled engine. The airworthiness of the Theiss *Speedster* could now be written off. Forward we go.

One of the ways to travel between Salem, (home base of Theiss Aviation) and Miller airport (location of the *Speedster*) was down Johnson Road. The route provided for a different landscape to be seen by those traveling almost daily from point to point. To the average person, it was just flat farm land. To the Theisses, it was perfect for a future airfield.

Then, behold! A posted sign announcing the available acreage to be auctioned off in something less than two weeks. Wow! The printed matter concerning the property even suggested that a certain twelve acres would be perfect for a landing strip. This had to be God's leading.

Having joined the other company officers in prayer over God's will, Shawn was in attendance for the sale of the large tracts of land. After bidding off a few of the subdivided tracts of land, the tract that Theiss Aviation had its eye on came up for auction. There were only a couple of individuals, Shawn included, that were bidding on this piece of land. Things were looking very promising. Then, just as it appeared that Theiss would have the winning bid, a local realtor made short order of the proceeding by buying the entire tract. This could have easily been a time of disappointment; however, Shawn felt led to make a date with Tanner Realty (the winning bidder) to discuss the realtor's plans for the property. The following day, the twelve acres suggested for a landing strip was to be set aside for Theiss Aviation. Now, how would God the Heavenly Father, arrange for the down payment? If the Theiss family had truly prayed for God's leading in this, then the answer would be provided.

GOD'S PLAN

In June of 1997, TEAM, producers of a fine line of ultralight and home-built aircraft kits, won a court battle in which an owner of one of their craft had been injured. The out-of-state flyer had sued the firm by contending that "inferior materials had been supplied in the kit." Most in the industry knew this to be untrue. However, divisive attorneys were not too hard to retain, and so armed, the case went forward.

The cost of defense was so great that when the beaten client appealed the verdict of the court, TEAM was forced to close up shop. Some sixty-five people were laid off. This, Shawn thought to himself, couldn't be happening. If the client built 51 percent of the kit, it was free from this kind of litigation; or so it was supposed to be under the law.

The issue played heavily on Shawn's mind. He had just issued the first kit (New Testament Bible packed within) to a customer in Akron, Ohio. To top it off, Ed Fisher (a noted aircraft designer and friend) had mentioned after first seeing the Speedster, "Someday you'll be attending an airshow, and there it will be—you're *Speedster* in air, show colors, ready to do its stuff."

Good heavens! Shawn thought, *It's an ultralight, not an aerobatic plane!* Someone could get hurt if they over stressed the craft. By virtue of its fitting within the parameters of ultralight FAA Part 103 specifications, the *Speedster* actually did not even require a licensed pilot. Now what?

In August of 1997, Volume 13, Number 8 of *Sport Pilot & Ultralights* magazine hit the newsstands of the world. In January of 1998, Theiss Aviation received a letter from Richard J. Foch, head of the Off-Board Countermeasures Division of the Naval Research Laboratory (NRL) in Washington, D.C. He had just read the article in Sport Pilot Magazine, and seemed interested in the construction method Theiss was utilizing in the ultralights (the Theiss construction method had been proven to not only be strong, easy to work with, and cost effective, but also able to absorb and dissipate harmonic vibrations like no other airframe construction methods). Revealing little more than interest, Mr. Foch closed by advising Theiss Aviation to expect a call from his office in the near future. That was it, nothing more.

A letter, such as it was, from a government agency was enough to set Richard off. "Oh man! What have we done now?" His only reasoning of the matter was that, "Perhaps we have encroached on something secret!" It was Richard himself who, a few weeks later, took the phone call from Rick Foch. He surely seemed nice enough as he invited the officers of Theiss Aviation to the Naval Research Laboratory; however, Richard still had his concerns. A date for the visit to NRL was made for the following Monday. He recommended a motel directly across from the entry to the navy base. The reason for the forthcoming meeting was still not clearly stated.

THEISS

AS A YOUNGSTER, SHAWN THEISS BUILT MODELS. NOW HE HAS DESIGNED A TRUE ULTRALIGHT WITH THE APPEARANCE OF A GOLDEN AGE RACER

AVIATION

BY NORM GOYER

I first met Shawn Theiss at the 1997 Sun 'n Fun EAA Spring Fly-In. I was attracted to his booth by the racing pylon set up in front which carried the Theiss Aviation banner and their motto: "Essence of the Past in Products of the Present."

Then I noticed the aircraft, in various stages of completion, parked under the canopy. For a moment, I thought I was seeing slightly smaller scale replicas of 1930s Thompson Trophy racers. The biplane with the top shoulder wing reminded me very much of the Knight Twister biplane. I wanted to get a closer look, so I worked my way through the crowd of people who'd also been attracted to the good-looking aircraft.

As a child, Shawn was building CO2-powered models of his full-size favorite airplanes some of which he'd seen at the local airport.

Eighteen worldwide aviation publications provided Theiss Aviation with a jump start.

On Sunday afternoon, contemplation and prayer were the order of the day as Shawn and Richard traveled to Washington to the hotel at which they would be meeting Rick the following morning.

Polite, pleasant, and most congenial were all attributes possessed by Richard J. Foch. Head of a government office or not, he was a real airman. How bad could that be? The sign-in process, the tour of the facilities; could all of this be really happening? And for that matter, what is happening? What exactly is NRL's interest in Theiss Aviation?

Dad Theiss once remarked to a friend, "After seeing the things we did during that first meeting, I will never again pooh-pooh the person that claims to have seen a UFO!"

The tour of the NRL complex gravitated towards the conference room. There, awaiting the Theiss officers, was a handpicked group of engineers and scientist involved with the day-to-day activities related to unmanned aircraft. Although the majority of them were young, each had garnered the title of doctor before their names. It was evident to both Richard and Shawn that they were seated among the brilliant of the research lab. The one thing that bound all in attendance was the fact that they were model airplane builders and flyers—a basic necessity to understanding flight. The first question asked of Shawn was, "what does it feel like to test an aircraft developed from new methods of design and manufactured materials?" Shawn lowered his head in contemplation of an answer. (Had he given it much thought before, he just may not have done the testing at all). Breaking the moment of silence, Richard said, "We pray a lot!"

The statement brought laughter from around the table, but, formed a basis for a Christian witness. It would soon be evident to all that for Theiss Aviation, prayer was the foundation upon which all design, construction, and flight was executed.

At day's end, the real reason for the (not by chance) meeting was presented. The UAVs being flown by the naval laboratory were packed with very expensive electronic equipment. Engine vibration and rough landings were often damaging to the flight systems and payloads. With Theiss products having the ability to dampen such, would the firm be interested in building UAVs for the Navy?

Remembering the moment, it was no small matter to appear calm, cool, and collected. Both president and vice president sensed a measure of success knocking at their hangar door (even if they didn't have one as yet).

The details of the new contract were hammered out the next day. In years to come, there would be many trips to and from the Washington, D.C. area. The Lord God and His Son Jesus were given full praise and credit all the way back to the waiting women in Salem. Hope and Shawn's intended (Charlene) had their ears filled with the details of the trip.

For Shawn, the real clincher to the deal was Rick Foch saying, "From the moment those planes roll out of your shop, the US Navy will assume all liability." He continued, "And if we crash one of them, we'll just pick up the phone and order another plane from you."

Thank you Jesus!

The final indication from Rick was that Theiss would be building about four aircraft per year. They (the laboratory) would fly and beat them up. Theiss would replace them as needed.

"Dad," Shawn flatly stated, "We're done building planes for general aviation!" he added, "From now on, its US government contracts only."

Easily said! What about the thirty some kits Bob Scott and his Texas friend were expecting? And, what about the ton of mail starting to come in as the result of Magazine articles worldwide?

A letter would have to be sent to all. Theiss Aviation Kits would no longer be available. All future efforts were to be directed toward the US department of defense.

God's plan was now being realized in its entirety. First, suitable property for the shop, hangar, and airfield had been found. Next, the magazine article had caught the eye of the Navy Research Lab, and the down payment for the first plane produced (plus the intent to order more aircraft), which was sufficient enough to obtain a small business loan for the procurement of the arranged property, and to start the construction on the new hangar.

Can anyone doubt the power and perfect timing of the Lord or his reward for faith? Time again for praising His name. And they did.

OFF IN A NEW DIRECTION

The first craft being developed for NRL was a joint venture between Theiss Aviation and the laboratory. The basic design layout was by Rick Foch himself. Structural design was performed by Shawn. Turning the eighteen foot spanned craft into a handy, foldable unit that could fit aboard a submarine was also the accomplishment of Theiss Aviation.

Although NRL would name the craft *Dakota II*, Theiss, realizing the potential market beyond the US Navy, named the craft the *Tarzan TD-1A*. A promotional brochure was soon developed that wove the name into the features of the UAV such as:

> Now, without further delay, you can swing into action with the lightweight, strong and agile Theiss Tarzan!

> And, for more information as to why the leaders in research have gone 'ape' over the Theiss Tarzan, contact...

When the wood framed, foam craft was ready for its fabric covering, Rick Foch and two of his staff flew out to northeast Ohio for an inspection. Rick's right hand man (Rudy Monteleone) and newest staff member (Eric Peddicord) soon proved essential to the inspection as they visually scanned every nook and cranny. It passed inspection.

Naval Research Lab team inspection of Theiss Tarzan.

Within ninety days of the first meeting with NRL, Theiss Aviation delivered their first Unmanned Air Vehicle. Its empty weight of sixty-five pounds was five pounds lighter than the requested maximum empty weight. (A plus for the Theiss team.) The second return trip from Washington, D.C. seemed even more blessed than the first as an order for two more UAV's was in hand.

Within a few days, Shawn tendered his resignation to the engineering department of the Electric Furnace Company. Theiss Aviation had finally become a full-time, working company, with an assembly line of two aircraft to boot.

The company's barn/shop was wall to wall with airplane parts—government on the first floor, sport planes and kits on the second.

In addition, Shawn was now able to acquire the bank loan necessary to purchase the future Theiss Field. Finally, they had their airfield. But at the present time, it was all literally a field. In fact, over the next couple of weeks, every free moment was spent with Shawn, Dad, Mom, and Charlene picking up every rock and stone they could find on the entire twelve acres. The small mountain of rocks still stands at the time of this writing. A tribute to the "rock-hard dedication" of the four

As progress was being made in the town shop, progress was slowly being made on the new hangar at Theiss Airfield. 1998 and 1999 brought brutal winters and exceptionally wet springs severe enough to delay the hangars completion, deeming that it being used as a manufacturing facility was far off.

"We'll insulate what we have and make it work." Shawn was a fighter, and he was on a roll.

This being only the firms second contract with the US government, there was still much to be learned. Those at the top of the contractual heap, in a whimsical moment, can wreak havoc far down the line of underlings. In this case, Theiss Aviation.

Somewhere up the line, a navy procurement officer declared that henceforth, all future UAV's that were to be used shipboard (i.e. the new *Dakota II*) would use heavy-fuel engines. The desire to reduce the danger of gasoline fires on-board ships could not be faulted, but the timing of the decree could not have been worse.

The basic difference between the first *Dakota II* and the second two was enough to designate the first version A, and the next two versions B. The first aircraft was fabric covered and had a fifteen horse powered gas engine. Version B was to be aircraft plywood covered and would now need to sport a physically larger diesel engine of twenty eight horse power.

Both craft (A and B) were designed with a twelve inch wide fuselage. However, the new requirement for the diesel engine would now call for a fuselage width of eighteen inches. Easy enough to do, as long as the request from NRL had come at the start of the project. Not contemplating the speed at which Theiss was building, both fuselages were already finished. The option of widening the fuselage at this point was unrealistic; to achieve the new width, two completely new fuselages would need to be constructed. There was neither the time nor the budget to do that. It was decided that a re-design from the firewall forward, including the cowling for the twenty eight horse power-plant, would have to do. With that, work proceeded.

Shawn would spend the last week of construction pushing himself to the limit in an effort to meet the contracted delivery schedule. For seventy-four hours straight, he would not sleep or leave the shop (other than to occasionally use the restroom), and would be sustained on coffee and cookies until the final bolt was tightened on the airframes. The aircraft were finished early in the morning two days before the craft were to be delivered; at this point, Shawn also was finished. He finally went to bed and slept for twelve hours before awakening to complete the saga.

Two more foldable craft for the U.S. navy.

As photos confirm, it could not have been colder on the morning that the two newly finished *Dakotas* were packed into the company's trailer. As timing would have it, Shawn would need to be in the Washington area on the Sunday before his scheduled delivery of the planes to NRL on Monday. Get Out and Push, the bluegrass band Shawn was playing bass with, was contracted to perform at the Washington National Press Club that Sunday evening. He made his delivery to NRL the next morning on time.

The spring season of 1999 brought about the completion of the new Theiss hanger, a place now to transfer the two sport planes, gazillions of kit-plane parts, and the materials for the next four *Dakota II* (*Tarzan*) aircraft yet to be ordered by the Naval Research Laboratory. In addition to the above, a newly acquired ultralight would also call Theiss Field home. A single-place *Weed Hopper* ultralight was to satisfy Shawn's urge to get back into the air with as little expense as possible.

The flying thing arrived initially at the Barn/Shop in two long blue cloth bags and totally confused the shippers. Shawn's explanation of an airplane inside only worsened their understanding.

A fixed base: home at last!

Unpacked and assembled, Shawn's mind went to work on the needed modifications. Yes, he still had to add his own touch to a design. The wing area would surely support two people. Richard would probably enjoy flying it too. Well, maybe not with that chair seat hanging out in space. As Shawn remembered, that's why he designed the ultralight sport planes in the first place. A pod fuselage was under way within a matter of hours.

By the time the craft was transferred to the flying field, it had a modified tail, a sleek, two-place pod fuselage, and ailerons (the original design only utilized rudder and elevator for flight controls). Being painted black and yellow, the neighboring farmers dubbed it,

Open air fun for the team.

As the *Wicked Weed* traveled from its home base to other airports throughout northeast Ohio, Shawn continued to experiment with different engine and prop combinations on the craft (always striving for performance perfection).

One frequent destination was to Koons airfield. This was where Shawn had crashed in his *Fisher 101* years before. The flying location was of importance to the Theiss clan for a number of reasons. The original owner, Kenny Koons, had since passed away, leaving the control of the field in the hands of his two sons, David and Harry.

David, a master of the paint gun, was responsible for the table top smooth finishes to be found on the Theiss *Tarzans*. Brother Harry was responsible for much of the facility construction going on at Theiss Field. The hangar and its future expansions would have Harry's finger prints all over them. Though both boys had been raised by Kenny to fly a variety of general aviation craft, David immediately took an interest in Shawn's *Fisher 101* ultralight, and had since then acquired a two-place *Quicksilver*. Shawn and David would attend many local fly-ins in the *Quicksilver* and *Wicked Weed*.

Back at Koons Field, a close friend of Richard, Frank Easton of *Flying Flea* fame, had rolled his small aircraft on a take-off attempt and the rebuilding of the craft had begun in the main hangar at Koons. Realizing that at his age, flying the *Flea* again would most likely not be advisable. Frank determined that the craft would be repaired to flying condition but then donated to the EAA Museum for all aviation enthusiasts to enjoy. Well aware of the Theiss accomplishments and abilities, Frank approached Richard and Shawn to aide in the small *Flea's* restoration. The restoration would be completed in the Theiss hangar two months later. From there, it was off to the EAA Museum in Oshkosh, Wisconsin.

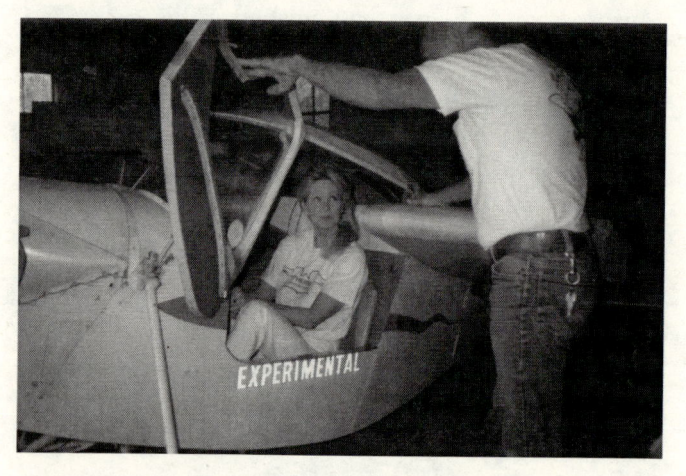

Hope (in French designed Flying Flea) talking with finisher David Koons.

The rare, famous, French-designed aircraft proved to be the link between Theiss Aviation and the man who would soon become Theiss Aviation's consultant to the US Military.

New to the Salem area, Dr. Robert Williams and his wife Patricia had just flown over the town with Harry Koons in a *Cessna 172*. While back in the Koons airport office, Bob noticed a photo of the *Flying Flea* and expressed both knowledge and interest in the craft. "Would you like to see the real thing?" asked Harry.

Richard was working on the plane when Bob and Pat walked into the hangar wearing big smiles. A lifetime friendship would begin at this point. A bonus for Theiss Aviation was the fact that Bob was actually Col. Robert Williams, Aero-Space surgeon (retired). He had flown standard engine aircraft, jets, and choppers. To top it all off, he was also A&E (aircraft and engine) maintenance trained.

Bob and Pat Williams—Theiss Aviation consultants to the U.S. military.

> From: Williams <rwilliams4@neo.rr.com>
> To: George.Gluski <George.Gluski>
> Date: Thursday, January 03, 2002 12:30 PM

Dear George,
This is to follow up on our conversation last night(01/02/02) to make sure you have our e-mail address: rwilliams4@neo.rr.com A packet of information will be on the way soon that you can pass along.
The Theiss Tactical UAV is a craft proven to be superior in its class. Its' cost is one tenth the cost of the current Pioneer System. It is also an extremely affordable system for the Boarder Patrol. It takes one man less than 3 minutes to set up this vehicle.
Thank you for your referrals to Ellis Golson at the DCD at Fort Rucker and the Combat Development Division at Fort Benning. We believe this UAV will be a tremendous tactical weapon while saving restricted budgets millions of dollars.
I hope to talk to you soon.

Best wishes to you&Peg,
Doc Williams

P.S. Richard Theiss can be reached at:
Theiss Aviation
P.O. Box 1086
Salem, OH 44460-1247
Office# (330) 332-2031

>-----Original Message-----
>From: Williams [mailto:rwilliams4@neo.rr.com]
>Sent: Sunday, January 13, 2002 5:35 PM
>To: Gluski, George COL NGB-ARNG

P.P.S. I will send this copy along in case I did not get your e-mail down accurately.

His all too brief association with Theiss Aviation (he was slowly dying with Lou Gehrig's disease) would open doors to former officer friends who had attained the rank of General. Pat also facilitated a smooth flow of information between Theiss Aviation and the military. Blessed are they who look to Him for all needs to be met.

The signs of the fall season just couldn't be better; schools were back in session, the Columbiana and Canfield County Fairs were on the roll, football season was underway, and the trees and bushes were ablaze with color. The air seemed easier to breath as the summer heat faded. Per usual, Hope was fall house cleaning, happy to have the many airplane parts transferred from her home to the hangar.

The phone rang. "Mrs. Theiss?" It was Eric Peddicord with the navy lab.

"Hi!" Hope answered, "How are things in Washington?" she asked.

"Don't know," said Eric, "I'm in California." He continued, "Is Shawn there?"

"No, the boys are at the airfield, and we don't have the phones in yet. Can I do something?"

"Yes, you can start praying because we are ready to test your airplanes." His voice contained a tinge of excitement.

"I'll do that Eric!" She committed herself.

"Talk later," *Click*. He hung up.

At that time, Hope did not know that the three navy aircraft with the Theiss logo on their tails had been transferred to a remote airstrip at Camp Roberts in central California. All she knew was that they were being flown for the first time. So she prayed.

All things considered, it was best that the designer/builder team was busy at other things. Just knowing that the flight tests were at hand would have caused a gnawing tenseness in both body and mind.

Richard once picked the mind of designer Rick Foch. "I'll bet you're relieved after the completion of the first test flight of one of your designs."

"No!" was Rick's short answer, "The second flight!" It made sense.

Within an hour from the time Eric had called, he called again. "Mrs. Theiss?"

"Yes!"

With even more excitement in his voice, he continued. "Boy, those prayers of yours really do pay off!"

All three craft had performed well. And not only well, they set a new altitude record for the range. Hope couldn't help feel that another witness had been given to the NRL test crew in California. God had indeed blessed again.

Praise God, They Fly!

Returning home that evening, Shawn and Rich joined Hope in her joy over the news from the west coast. Thus inspired, it was decided to start work on the next four *Tarzans* even though the lab had not yet officially placed the order for them.

As winter set in, the fuselage parts were started in the basement of the house in Salem (the new hangar did not have a heating system yet). In time, they joined the other Theiss products in the new hangar shop at Theiss field.

As flight data started to come in from the navy test flight crew in California, the Theiss team began to realize the full potential of their first UAV offering. The standard for their optimism was based on a craft being used by the US Navy for the past some eighteen years.

The *Pioneer* was a single winged, twin-tail boomed, single engine, pusher UAV. It was basically made of fiberglass and was launched from the deck of ships by the use of a catapult and JATO (jet assisted take off) systems.

Product Comparison between the Pioneer UAV and TARZAN Dokota II		
	Conventional Pioneer	Affordably Expendable Tarzan
Launch Options	Ground/Ship	Ground/Ship
Wingspan (Ft.)	16.8	18.8
Length (Ft.)	14.0	10.0
Empty Weight (Lbs)	450	260
Payload Area (Cubic Ft.)	1	8
Payload (Lbs)	50	90
Take-off Distance (Ft.)	1,800	200
Climb Rate (Ft. per min.)	400	750
Endurance (Hrs.)	6	7
Cruise Speed (Kts.)	60	53
Cost (Airframe+Engine+Avionics)	$667,000	$70,000

Until the advent of the Theiss *Tarzan*, the *Pioneer* had the government market cornered. Surely, when the Secretary of the US Navy (Danzig) had become aware of the comparatives, he would choose the Theiss product hands down. Along that line of thinking, Shawn prepared the following:

The *Pioneer* was a product of Israel. At some point in time, the plane was still produced overseas, but was assembled in the US. Clearly, there was much to be made by all concerned with the procurement process.

Rick Foch also published the performance results and saw to it that Secretary Danzig had a copy in his confidential files. But still, there was no response.

Not one to sit on his hands, Shawn went to Washington and met with Congressman Jim Traficant. The Democrat from Northeast Ohio was known as a no nonsense representative. And he proved to be.

The Theiss Aviation president returned with a most beautifully made American flag and the promise to contact the navy's secretary ASAP.

In less than a week, a copy of a letter mailed to Secretary Danzig was received. It stated that as a steward of the American tax dollar, he (Traficant) wanted to know why the navy was still buying the foreign made, overpriced, inferior *Pioneer*, while the American made *Tarzan* was clearly the better deal. As before, there was no response.

The fact that Secretary Danzig was a Clinton appointee made little difference to Traficant. Eventually, it was the Congressman's refusal to keep in step with the Democratic Party that cost him his position.

In the meantime, it was becoming increasingly clear that the navy research lab would have to default on their verbal intent for four more *Tarzans*.

The current occupant in the US Whitehouse loathed the military and was doing his best to shut down bases and cut off as much spending in its behalf as possible. In a way, Theiss Aviation (and any other Department of Defense contractors) seemed to be in his political gun sights. This, and activities within the oval office that were corrupting the youth of America, prompted Hope Theiss to write to the US president.

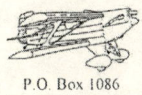

THEISS AVIATION

P.O. Box 1086
Salem, Ohio 44460

Phone:
(216) 332-2031

Dear Mr. President:

As a concerned christian and citizen of the U.S.A.
I see the U.S. headed down a very disturbing path.

In taking a look at the downfall of the Roman Empire
I see some very similar traits. In reviewing Edward
Gibbon in his classic work " The Decline & Fall of the
Roman Empire", he gave five key reasons for Romes downfall.
1. The undermining of the dignity and sanctity of
    the home.
2. Increasing taxes and spending of public money for
    bread and circuses.
3. The mad craze for pleasure, with sports becoming
    more exciting and more brutal.
4. The building of gigantic armaments, when the _real_
    enemy is the decadence of the people.
5. The decay of religion, with faith fading into mere
    form.
Do those sound familiar, Mr. President?

From the first years of Americans' history, the founding
fathers acknowledged God's providence and recognized
that the nations destiny was in His hands. But today
we see His name being dishonored, His standards of right
and wrong mocked, and His claims ignored. As a result,
some of the same traits that sapped the power of the Roman
empire are slowly draining our nations strength.

So what can christian citizens of the U.S. or of any other
country do to preserve their nation from decline? We
should tell others about Christ and the importance of faith
in God.. We also need to _stand_ up for truth and justice
and call for our leaders to rule according to righteousness.
But can we relie on them?

History's lesson is clear; No nation can long endure whose
God is not the Lord. As stated in Psalma 33:12 " Blessed is
the nation whose God is Jehovah".

Mr. President as you are so good at quoting the great men of
ole...I'm sure you'll remember who said these words of wisdom..
" IT IS IMPOSSIBLE TO RIGHTLY GOVERN THE WORLD WITHOUT GOD AND
  THE BIBLE". That Mr. President was George Washington. So
please pray with us for God to grant wisdom and strength to all
who serve our countrys needs, then God will forgive our sins and
heal our land, that is a promise He gives us. We plead this in
Jesus name.

Thank you Mr. President for taking the time to read this and my
prayer is that you too will join us in prayer for our new leaders
comming up in January.

Yours in Christ

Hope Theiss

Essence of the Past in Products of the Present

Having cleared the air (for her) on the political scene, Hope now turned her attention to the firm's president and his intended. Shawn and Charlene were going to be married.

Shawn requested that his father be his best man and Charlene's mother was to be her maid of honor. Almost befitting of royalty, the wedding and reception were flawless, and the celebration of uniting the two was enjoyed by over 250 guests! With this, another responsibility was added to the list for the youngest of the Theiss clan. But there was no doubt about it; if anyone could handle it, he could!

Returning from his honeymoon, Shawn soon launched into an effort to broaden his firm's ability to satisfy the UAV market with more than just aircraft having a span of eighteen feet and weighing in at 150 pounds. Indeed, Shawn was confident that his design experience could satisfy any size aircraft required by the U.S. Department of Defense. As Jack Hood, senior artist manager with Walt Disney, once said, "If Shawn designed and built it, it'll fly!"

In time, Shawn was led to a Florida based firm, named Micro Systems. In turn, members of that firm suggested that Texas based Tom Prescott of Prescott Products, Inc. be brought into the mix. He (Prescott) was active with military contracts and had contacts in Washington D.C. Apparently, Tom could show Shawn the ropes when it came to government dealings.

With the uncertain future of military spending looming overhead, Shawn might have just thrown up his arms and returned to the life of designing for the general public. However, with the responsibility of another mouth to feed, he phoned Prescott.

Tom certainly seemed to be a man of certain ways and means in Washington. But, as expected, it would cost to tap into the inner workings of his mind and connection system. This would require some reassessment of available funds by Shawn. Little time was spent in the effort as there were no funds available for any such retainer.

The lack of said funds in the company was the result of monthly payments due for the small business loan on the airfield property, its hangar/shop building, tools and machinery that now occupied much of the floor and wall space, new work benches, tables, and storage bins. Also, the purchase of materials to build four, wide-body *Tarzans* that now had no home. In addition to plumbing installation was the electrical and heating systems installation, followed by monthly utility bills.

Then, wouldn't you know, Bill Blohm (the old Connecticut neighbor who had purchased the unfinished prototype *Sportster* ultralight), apparently figured that he might be too old and inexperienced to handle the small agile plane and wanted to sell it back to the firm. Hope did a deep dip into her personal account and sent Bill happily on his way. With the cancellation of the order for the four additional *Tarzans* and no new contracts to provide any income for the young company, the well was near dry. Not a comforting thought for the head of office activities. Prayer was offered, and God's will was sought after.

A FAMILY AFFAIR

The four offspring of Richard and Hope split into two distinct groups of two and two. The two older children were of mild temperament and were most content to work for others. They loyally served whomever and whatever seemed worthy of their attention. The younger two were seldom content to follow, and would claw and push towards the top of whatever task was at hand. Though honesty and fairness were core values, their sights were always set on success. Always of comfort to their parents was the evident love and caring between all four children, despite the differing personalities.

If there was one person on all of planet earth who understood the drive and mental workings of Shawn, it was his sister, Michelle. She, by sheer personal strength, endless hours of work, passion for success, and a faith in the one who could bring it all to pass, had climbed to a position of prominence with a worldwide leader in telecommunication services, MCI. Michelle had just returned from Russia, and was currently handling capital contracts in the central south section of the US for the firm.

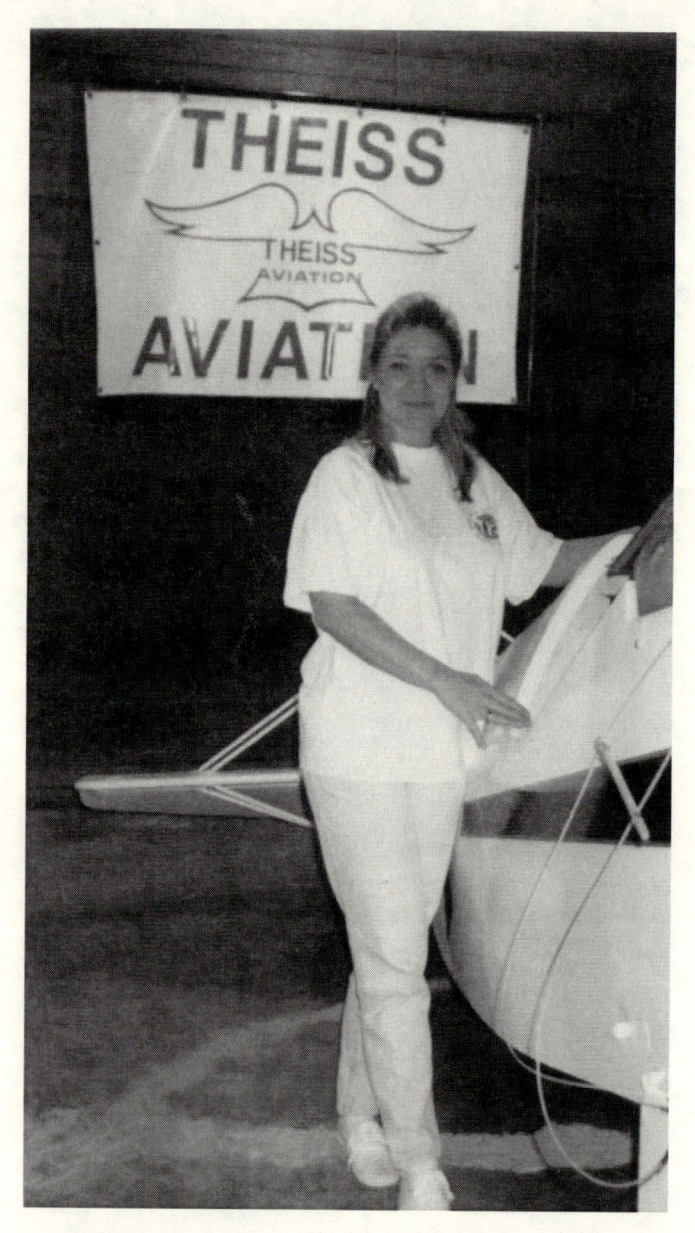

Sister Michelle on a Theiss Aviation factory visit.

She and Shawn were both "outside of the box" thinkers and planners.

Being Christian, each branch of the family shared praises and problems with each other—this was to petition prayers for all. Family wise, it was no secret; Theiss Aviation was badly in need of funds if they were to survive the current lack of work and subsequent cash flow problem.

All avenues were considered. Close, successful friends suggested going public. Others said borrow from the banks, the rich and famous, or investment groups. After all, who from among us would turn down such a noble effort as designing and building UAVs for the good of the American government? The list of turn downs could fill a not too small book. Oh, there was money to be had, just as long as Shawn was willing to turn control of the firm over to a manager sent.

Oh, sure! That would work—for about as long as it took for Shawn to turn the deal down. There was no way Theiss Aviation would take the path of Piper, Taylorcraft, or Stinson on their way to near oblivion over the need for cold, hard cash.

Enter his sister, Michelle.

"How much do you need?" she asked.

"About fifteen thousand!" Shawn answered.

"You've got it!"

Within a few days, Shawn received a card. The note accompanying the check simply stated, "Go for it!"

With the indication of money in hand, Tom Prescott started spewing forth the how-to's when trying to impress the many offices of the US Government,

NASA, DARPA, the FAA, etc. Though the connection was never really established, Tom also knew of an army project that had been well funded, but with poor results.

The project named "Back Pack" was for a small UAV (thirty-six-inch span) equipped with an up/down real time video link (camera and monitor). All this was to fit into a box that was ten inches by twenty inches by forty inches. After some two years, the contractor was unable to come up with a flyable craft that would meet the army's requirements. This was unthinkable to the Theisses. Apparently, the US Army had more than a million dollars to throw at anyone who might claim to have some ability with flying things.

Without hesitation, Shawn launched into an answer for the army's needs. Within a few weeks, he had produced a foldable, double winged UAV that resembled a nasty looking flying bomb. At this stage of development, there was no question about it. It would fly.

The size of the box was most adequate for the containment of both the aircraft and the rest of the required gear. "Okay army, here we come!"

Theiss Aviation now had two craft to peddle; one large *Tarzan* and the brand new smaller *Viper*. To Shawn, the name seemed proper for the craft that could surely strike a surveillance blow to the enemy.

Vipers for the U.S. army "Backpack" program.

    A number of trips were made to National offices located in Washington D.C. by Shawn and Tom Prescott. They met and talked with reps from the Army's War Office, as well as those representing the US Department of Agriculture. All seemed to have an interest in both aircraft and promised to look into the possibilities of their future use.

    Washington talk was cheap, but not so was Prescott's travel or tutor's fee. It didn't take the company's accountant long to see that once again, the green was running short.

The slack in the effort to find a new government contract was now taken up by Colonel "Doc" Williams. His goal was to locate the illusive army's "Back Pack" program. Calls were made to any and all who might shed some light on the subject. Here again, no one really knew the status of the program. Apparently, the lack of a flyable craft by the project contractor brought about the grounding of the project; hence why no one could offer Theiss Aviation any direction. How could this happen in America? Don't ask! "Okay, Lord. Now what?"

Well, how about a new baby girl. And, a move to a farm house that was a bit closer to Theiss Airfield. So now there is a third mouth to feed in Shawn's household, as well as a new house, but still no income through Theiss Aviation. The word of God clearly states that a man must provide for his family. Shawn started looking.

Some time was spent with a cemetery providing pre-need sales. Though not a profession Shawn had had previous experience in, nor a profession that he saw as long term, it did meet the immediate financial needs. With concern for whoever might hire him, Shawn would not become involved in a profession that would depend totally on his presence, for he knew that when Theiss Aviation received its blessings, he would be gone. But the Lord's time was not yet.

As before, the Master of all was bringing about the needed answers for both Shawn and (many miles away in Texas) his sister, Michelle. MCI was going through a buyout attempt, and Michelle and her husband, Roger, were no longer gracing the firm's office space.

Michelle had quickly been retained by a small but successful telecommunications engineering firm called OSP Consultants. Her credentials and years of experience in the industry vaulted Michelle up the corporate ladder within the company. Now, as the manager of the Midwest regional office, Michelle continued to succeed in her field of work. Ironically, one of her many clients was none other than her former employer. But as her client base grew, so did the work load for her small engineering office. She was in dire need of competent employees; she was in dire need of another engineer.

Prayers were offered, meetings were held, decisions were made, and in the fall of 2000, Shawn and his family would move to the Dallas, Texas area. Richard and Hope would keep an eye on the plant and airfield, and Shawn would continue to run all Theiss activities from Plano, Texas while simultaneously performing telecommunications engineering for his sister Michelle and OSP Consultants.

NOW WAS HIS PERFECT TIME!

Routines were being established. On the home front, Hope took and transferred calls as if Shawn were just an office away. At Theiss field, Richard had been mowing more grass than he had ever seen in one place. Maybe there was more than one reason for hard-surfaced runways!

As timing would have it, Shawn and his family had been in Texas for less than a year, and things with Theiss Aviation were potentially starting to get busy again. Micro Systems in Florida had been in contact with Shawn about a new military contract in the mill. Its code name was "Have Gold Three."

The primary contractor, the Shafer Corporation, was developing a missile defense system, and Theiss had been recommended as the builder of the test platforms. Shawn accepted; now the wide-bodied *Tarzan* could strut its stuff!

The next few months were a blur of activity. The telecommunication industry was expanding like wildfire, which kept the engineering firm very busy. Shawn was negotiating the contract and details of the "Have Gold Three" project, and Shawn, Charlene, and baby Josette had finally become firmly planted in a growing Christian fellowship. Shawn was playing drums and bass in the praise band, and Charlene was being prepped for the sound system control board (as with her previous camera work, she would be good at this). Lord, was a return to Ohio already necessary?

Much to the chagrin of Richard, Shawn and his wife were looking at homes and land for relocating Theiss Aviation down to the Dallas area. The idea went far enough as to place a "For Sale," real estate sign next to the entry gate of Theiss Field. Many were the times the vice president would pause at the gate long enough to ask God for the kind of business that would demand Shawn's return.

Work wise, Richard spent time in the old shop barn at 1100 Franklin Avenue in Salem, producing the leading edge of a radial cowling for the *Speedster* prototype. Shawn always did love round-engined airplanes. Not long before the relocation to Texas occurred, Shawn had been toying with the idea of upping the horsepower in the *Speedster*. Along those lines, a used sixty-five horsepower, German-built, Hirth Aircraft engine had been located, purchased, and was waiting for installation. Maybe this would help with Shawn's return.

Little did Richard realize at the time that the new radial cowling to the Theiss *Speedster* would be but one of many reasons for Shawn to return to the shop located in northeastern Ohio.

In mid 2001, the Ohio office received a call from a California firm that was immediately transferred to Shawn in Texas. The west coast based, American firm, Asian Funding Company was looking to satisfy an expressed need for the Commerce Department of

China to film remote areas of the nations northwest region. The desired results or further intent of the aerial activity was not stated. As with the "Have Gold Three" project, the Theiss *Tarzan* was being considered as the flight platform to do the job.

The next few weeks were intense with negotiations between Shawn and the representatives of both the American firm and the Chinese. The pending deal was mind boggling. The Chinese would buy two hundred of the eighteen foot spanned craft, but with one stipulation: Any further craft would be built in China under license from Theiss Aviation.

For the small, Ohio-based firm, this was a potential contract greater in magnitude than anything previously experienced. This was surely a time for calling on the Master of the Universe for guidance and direction.

First, a family member attorney with a large Pittsburgh law firm was consulted. Would a contract with China be approved by the US Government? After all, these aircraft were designed for surveillance, and the potential customer had a history with secret operations in military arenas. Of question too was the large number required (considering the money involved, this concern was not too vigorously pursued).

Welcomed was the answer as to US government approval of the pending contract. By coincidence, other military craft were being built in China under contract to a parent American firm. This showed that the possible use of the Theiss craft for surveillance was all right by the US.

With the apparent government approval to deal with China in this matter, the next step would be to physically gear up for production; an expansion of the *Tarzan* assembly line would be in order. This would require another, larger structure to the east of the current Theiss hangar. In addition, the hiring of a work force to handle the new production line would be necessary. But, what was to become of them when the two hundred craft were completed? How often would contracts of this size come by? First things first. Richard was on his knees at the shop, and Hope stayed close to the phone in Salem; both were in constant prayer.

Shawn was the recipient of their petitions as he put the finishing touches on the contract. Now it was in the Chinese court of play. Would they agree to the Theiss terms? The tension of the moment was eased a bit by the cooler fall days that had arrived with the end of August. *What a grand fall season this will be*, thought Richard as he removed the "For Sale" sign at the entry gate to Theiss field.

Yes! The time had come; God was answering his prayers. Although Shawn and his family would not be returning just yet, it had been decided that with the pending "Have Gold Three" project and the Chinese contract, Theiss field was to be the firm's primary place of business forever more. Great is His faithfulness! Finally, the call from Texas revealed that Shawn would be flying to California for the signing of the contract early the following week.

Now the conversation turned to the expected travel to China so as to set up the *Tarzan* production line for the continuance of the contract. Shawn would be going first, then Richard and Hope would follow some time later.

A new prayer request was issued by the company's president. Although he and his vice president were both lifetime, free-flight, model aircraft builders and flyers, it would take someone with a lot of experience in radio control flying to handle the Tarzan. Remember, to date, NRL had been the only customer of the *Tarzan*, and they had performed all of the initial test flights with their own UAV pilots. Where on earth could Theiss Aviation find a pilot such as that to perform test flights and provide UAV pilot training for the customers? Answer—prayer!

A lady friend and sister in the church had been dating a gentleman who had a friend who had been a UAV pilot in the navy, was currently in the navy reserve, and lived just minutes away from Theiss field. Was that all? No! He was also a born-again Christian. Praise the Lord time!

Tom Zets, as it turned out, was one of the navy's first three *Pioneer* pilots, and had a blue blood résumé of flight activity of over some nineteen years of service. "Please give him a call!" Shawn was insistent.

A CHANGED WORLD

It was morning. The sun would be rising about one hour earlier over northeast Ohio than it would be over the Dallas, Texas area.

As Richard left the house for the shop, Hope reminded him of his Class of '48 breakfast at ten o'clock that morning. "I'll meet you there. Don't be late!" she added.

Per usual, he had in fact forgotten what day the breakfast was and had left the lawn tractor in the shop hangar the day before (the lawn tractor served mowing duty at both their house, and at Theiss Field). In less than fifteen minutes the mower was loaded into the pickup truck, and he was again locking the main gate. As he headed back toward Salem, he turned on the radio.

Unlike Ohio, it was still hot in Texas, and Shawn was happy to be heading for an air conditioned office at OSP Consultants.

Catching bits and pieces over the radio, someone in the OSP office turned on the TV in the reception area, and froze with the site of a tall building belching huge plumes of black smoke. Soon, others in the office gathered to gaze in disbelief. This was (according to the excited commentator's voice) one of the twin towers located in the center of New York City.

A commercial aircraft had crashed into it for what seemed to be no logical reason. But, there it was, greatly damaged and vastly aflame.

Five hundred miles to the west of the burning building, Richard was listening to the radio's version of the results of the crash that had occurred but a short time before. In his mind, Richard was reminded of the time when a B-25 Air Corps bomber had crashed into the Empire State building many years before. Unlike the recent event, the bomber had spattered itself against the firm concrete side of the structure. But in this case, the transport had penetrated the famous tower and exploded inside the structure. *Good heavens! How could anyone survive? This thing was a flying bomb!* thought Richard.

By the time Richard met Hope at the class breakfast, the second aircraft had hit the second tower and his classmates were talking about at least two more airliners involved in what was shaping up to be a well organized terrorist attack. This tragic event would be known as the turning point that changed the course of America and, eventually, Theiss Aviation.

The events of September 11, 2001 were an unexpected, rude awakening to the fact that the United States still had many enemies in this world. And the effects of that brutal attack would be far reaching in many ways, some unknown immediately.

Some will argue that one of the near-term effects was the direct financial downfall of the telecommunications industry. For years, the industry had been highly inflated; money was spent like water. Some believe that the terrorist attack was enough to instill fear and lack of confidence in the economy long enough to push the teetering telecom industry over the edge. Regardless of the validity of this perspective, there was no doubt that stock values were falling within the major telecommunication companies, and the proverbial ship was sinking fast!

Seeing the eminent decline, the owners of OSP Consultants figured they better get what they could out of the company quickly, and then get out! Within a few short months, regional managers and engineers in every location were being cut loose from the company. Eventually, Michelle too received her notice. Shawn and another engineer stayed on as long as possible. But within two months of Michelle's leaving the company, the office was closed, and OSP Consultants was no more.

Though the telecommunication industry was suffering, Shawn remained calm as he knew that in the very near future, the Chinese contract and the Have Gold Three project would more than pick up the financial slack. Wanting to keep the ball rolling with both of these projects, he called the funding firm to verify final details for the signing of the Asian contract.

"With the current situation, we are on hold at this point." stated the agent. "You understand." he added.

"Of course!" Shawn agreed; what else could he do? He then emailed the Have Gold Three program manager and received the same "hold pattern" response. This status would continue for the next four weeks. Though not in a complete state of panic yet, Shawn was not as calm as he was just a few weeks before. Mindful of the Theiss connection with the navy's Washington-based, research lab, Shawn asked Richard to place a call to Rick Foch to see if there were possibly any UAV needs on their end. Time passed—there was no response from NRL.

It was learned (much later) that on September 11th, Rick Foch had suffered a heart attack in a cab while on the way to the airport. As a result, he missed his booked flight… a flight that would have taken him directly into the offices of the Pentagon (though not through any open doors)!

Yes, the all-loving, all-protecting God of the vast universe had saved the life of one Rick Foch; that he might continue a blessed association with the firm of Theiss Aviation. Talk about track records, our God is always there!

In an effort to keep the cash flow going, Shawn quickly began to consider other employment options around the Dallas area. A search for employment lead to a local company named Guardian Packaging—a firm with component supplier contracts with both Boeing and Lockheed Martin—that was in need of a floor manager to oversee production for these clients. "Well, it did have something to do with aircraft," Shawn mused. Though Shawn was highly overqualified for the position, he convinced them that they would not be exploiting him, and began work within two days of the preliminary interview.

The time spent at Guardian Packaging could not have been more stressful. New Job, new responsibilities, ongoing bills and family to feed, uncertain future for his own firm and its ongoing obligations. Most appropriate for a Christian at this time was Shawn's wondering what he would do if it weren't for Christ in his life. Who could he turn to? And what results could he expect?

Much relief from the worldly pressures came through an association with a newly formed, local Christian fellowship church. Shortly after joining, Shawn found himself in the praise band, and Charlene was being prepped as the new sound board technician (she would be good at this). Of benefit too were the shared prayer concerns for Theiss Aviation (that Shawn would most certainly believe in and expect results from).

Not wanting to get caught off guard when the two pending UAV contracts (Asia and "Have Gold Three") were ready to move forward, the Theiss Aviation officers agreed to pursue an arrangement with Tom Zets (the local UAV Pilot) for flying the craft. A date was made to sit down and talk more with Tom and his wife. Shawn flew back to Salem for the meeting. Also present were Christian sister, Annie Hubbard, and her finance, Doug (friend of Tom).

A Christian bond was quickly formed between the Theiss and Zets families. So far, the Theiss firm was 100 percent Christian, and this new business arrangement would only serve to continue that tradition. At the meeting, two VCR tapes provided more than just entertainment; Tom's tape displayed his flying skills both onboard ships and on land at a Naval airstrip.

Shawn's tape gave Tom his first look at the Theiss aircraft he would be flying.

Quite naturally, prayer for the company's future ended the meeting, and all parted ways feeling blessed.

The thing about praying for God's guidance is that the path revealed may not always be the path you envisioned. Some weeks later, it was fully realized that the dream deal with the Chinese would never be. Once again, political trends would be the demise of the small aviation firm. What could be learned from the hoped for effort?

In retrospect, the *Tarzan* design had qualified to do whatever job the Chinese had in mind. No legal fees had yet been incurred. No building expansion. No hiring. No... Hey, God just closed the door. Praise Him!

They still had the Have Gold Three project to look forward to, didn't they? Fast forward a couple weeks later—Theiss Aviation would also learn that the Schaffer project of Have Gold Three would also be cancelled due to the current state of the country. At a time when one would think that UAVs would be one of the hottest Department of Defense wish-list items, all of Theiss Aviation's potential UAV contracts were disappearing. Why was the government not pursuing UAV assets? They were, simply, not in the same direction as previously pursued.

So two doors were closed, but others were being opened.

An official letter from the US Naval Research Laboratory revealed an upcoming industry day for a new UAV project, and Theiss Aviation was invited to take part.

The US Marines, in conjunction with the navy, would be looking for bids to manufacture a small UAV to be utilized as an over-the-hill surveillance platform. The project, known as Dragon Eye, would be presented in Washington (at NRL) within a month's time. Shawn would again fly to the home office, and then drive to Washington with his VP. It would be the first time they would see Rick Foch since 9/11. Spirits were up as the time for the industry day approached.

Although Shawn's days were packed full with both his obligations to Guardian and the handling of Theiss Aviation's activities, Richard (on the other hand) found time to catch up on some reading; on aviation of course.

Dr. Bob and Patricia Williams kept the elder Theiss well stocked with relevant flying publications. It was in one such volume that Richard read of DARPA (Defense Advanced Research Projects Agency) looking for answers to the need for a very small UAV that could emulate a dragonfly or humming bird. The tiny flying thing would have to be rugged enough to withstand battle front conditions. *They must be kidding!* thought Richard.

The accompanying photo showed a small cast, aluminum airplane whose propeller was almost as large as the stubby wings. It fit into the palm of a human hand. Of course, they must be kidding! The object couldn't possibly fly, even if it were thrown like a rock! He read on.

Engineers were discovering that something strange would occur with craft having spans of less than six inches. The wings were much too small to sustain flight, at least the kind of flight hoped for; slow and manageable. This was because the aerodynamics game changed completely at those smaller scales and low airspeeds. Reynolds numbers and drag coefficients did not act anything like they do in larger flying things.

"Good heavens!" The loud proclamation shocked Hope as Richard sat up-right in bed. Shawn had the answer years ago. It was the McDonalds foam hamburger box that flew so perfectly at the indoor model meet at Glastonbury, Connecticut.

A quick scan of the magazines first pages revealed that the six-year-old publication was in its third printing. Apparently six years later, DARPA still had not determined why micro-sized planes couldn't fly as needed. "Because they had the shape of standard aircraft!" Richard stated to his half asleep, bewildered wife.

The next morning, Richard prepared a writing for review by Shawn. Soon they both agreed that the success of the hamburger box was due to its unconventional shape. It was not that of a standard airplane. The shape confounded all as it was a blunt, unconventional shape, yet it was stable and controllable in flight. Its flying body wedged through the thin air. Thick, aerodynamically-designed, bluff bodies would be DARPA's answer, not thin standard looking wings.

For Shawn , the conversation during the ride to Washington was most invigorating. Shawn would be writing DARPA just as soon as they returned from the Dragon Eye industry day.

RUBBING ELBOWS WITH THE BIG BOYS

After a good night's rest at the motel, the Theiss team relived what had become a ritual of entry to the NRL facility. First was the filling out of forms and registration to be confirmed by Rick Foch himself. Then a vehicle placard was placed in the car window for identification by the guard shack. Then, they headed off to the complex designated for the Industry Day presentation.

Once again, registration was required before entering the conference room, and a badge was issued to be worn by the guests.

Unlike former visits to the lab, Shawn and Richard were shown to a room adjacent to the entry lobby.

The room was filling up with expensively suited executives whose name tags revealed their respective firms—Lockheed Martin, General Dynamics, Sikorsky, Boeing, Raytheon, BAI, Northrop Grumman, and Aerovironment, just to name a few.

Well, the Theiss Aviation, Inc. representatives were decently dressed, and their name tags were as large as those seated around them. And besides, they knew Rick Foch who was principal investigator for the Dragon Eye project. This had to give them an upper hand, yes?

The latter fact did little to influence the letting of the contract, and shortly after the industry day had passed, Aerovironment along with BAI ended up as the two production firms chosen by the marines for the initial development of the craft. Of little consolation was Rick informing Shawn (at a later date) that Theiss had come in on the bidding at about mid point with the ten other firms.

Hey! You win some, and you lose some; the door does swing both ways.

And so it was when Shawn returned once again to his office in Texas. The opened door was by way of a government prime contractor named Lear Siegler, whose main office location was on the inside of an airship hangar at Lakehurst, New Jersey.

A quote for a system capable of carrying a fifty pound payload for two to three hours was requested. Further questions were asked about the system, delivery schedules were discussed, then a Theiss *Tarzan* was ordered (signed contract in hand). The hushed program was to be shared by both the US Army and CECOM. The data on the payload was minimal, and so, no further questions were pursued on the part of Theiss Aviation.

That did it! Shawn, Charlene, and baby Josette would be moving back to the Salem area. Of course, the VP and secretary-treasurer were happy beyond expression.

They (Richard and Hope) had recently sold the big house and moved from Salem to the south, some eight miles. The new gated community at the lake was known as Seven Springs. Shawn would stay in Texas for about a month more to wrap-up a project for Guardian, and to accumulate a little more cash for the move back to Ohio. His family would travel back ahead of him, and would be staying with the elder Theisses until Shawn joined them to find a home of their own. Within a few months, the two Theiss families became neighbors; Shawn's new home would also be in the gated community some two hundred yards to the north of Richard and Hope.

The small size of Theiss Aviation in relation to other aircraft builders smacked blunt in the face of Richard one evening while reading the local newspaper. There, on page one, was a picture of a Boeing UAV with a flattering caption. It read as if Boeing were the only firm producing unmanned aircraft.

"Fooey!" thought Richard. "Our craft can do the same things and for millions of dollars less!" True enough. But Boeing had two things that Theiss Aviation lacked—money and a promotion department. Accumulation of money was evidently not one of Richard's attributes. However, who said that a good promotional department had to be of a large size?

The first call made by the prospective new department was to the president. Shawn concurred that, indeed, this was something that the company needed if they were to continue to compete in this industry. Theiss Aviation now had a publicity department of one.

The next call was to Larry Shields, feature writer for the *Salem News*. Shields, with a photographer in tow, was permitted to enter the windowless factory. The result was a full, two-page feature in the Sunday edition—and in color, no less!

The areas readers were stunned to learn that those unmanned airplanes they would occasionally hear about on the news were being designed and built for the US government right under their noses

Larry Shields was good. He made it sound as if the mystique enjoyed by Lockheed's Skunk Works was also in full evidence on Johnson Road just north of Sebring, Ohio.

Traffic slowed slightly as it passed the small, blue building located next to the grass strip, with the wind sock giving indication that "this must be it!"

The phone started ringing. "Would it be possible for the *Morning Journal* to do a story on Theiss Aviation?" a writer asked.

Next was the *Alliance Paper*, then the *Canton Repository*. Factory tours by writers always gave the same results; full page, color features in the Sunday editions.

A Youngstown television station (WFMJ) was also granted an interview. As the anchorwoman sent her cameraman off with Shawn to obtain some good footage, she picked up a copy of *The Daily Bread* devotional from Shawn's desk. The title of that day's message caught her eye, and the Spirit moved in her. She began to cry. As she told of a close friend who had just passed away that morning, Shawn and Richard had the opportunity for a Christian witness. The Lord had led her to them in her time of need. He had provided the firm with the chance to build Christian relationships, not just aircraft.

The Theiss Aviation portion of that evenings broadcast brought about a date with yet another newspaper, *The Youngstown Vindicator*. Previous newspaper publications had spawned interest from other news papers and TV stations, as well as individuals seeking employment with the new found local, high-tech firm. However, the latest article would open the next door. *The Vindicator's* Sunday, feature article was read with interest by consultant Dave Nestic of Columbus, Ohio. Dave was visiting his mother-in-law in Salem for the weekend when he first read of the small company.

The Columbus based firm that Dave consulted for, Guild Associates, was a company that specialized in the development and production of chemical detection and decontamination equipment for the military. They had been watching the government's move towards small, UAV assets for some time. Guild wanted to get in on the new movement, but possessed no means of designing, building, or even flying a UAV. In addition, the Wright Patterson Air Force Research Laboratory (AFRL) in Dayton had just released an announcement to industry that they wanted a UAV system capable of detecting lethal gases.

Guild could provide the chemical sensors, and even had the ability and experience to be lead on the contract, but they were still missing a critical component. They needed a UAV company to design, build, and fly an aircraft capable of carrying their lethal gas detection equipment. It was also a desire to have all team members located in Ohio; especially with the project to be flown at Wright Patterson Air Force Base in Dayton, Ohio. Enter Theiss Aviation.

Initially, all correspondence and agreements between the two companies were by phone or email. Because of the rush to put a winning proposal together, Shawn would not actually meet the Guild team members until after the proposal was finished and been submitted to AFRL. After a one month review period, Guild associates received confirmation from AFRL that they had successfully won the contract.

The first task in the project was to assess the UAV industry to determine the best-fit airframe and autopilot system to utilize in the flight tests. It had been determined that Shawn would act as the principal investigator of available craft and systems to be considered for the project.

"Hey!" he spoke up at one of the initial meetings. "If as a designer and producer of small UAVs I am to determine which craft is to be used, is it still possible for me to compete in the bid process?"

"Of course!" was the quick answer. "We are relying on your experience to properly assess each craft being considered regardless of who produces it."

Right answer! Shawn quietly concluded in his mind.

Being taken into the bidding process at a later date, Richard enjoyed an interesting perspective. Shawn, having insight as to where the project needs lie, studied the relevant Theiss airframes and concluded that even though the two craft (the *Viper* and *PLANC*) might well fly the project, a design of specific intent would even be better.

The Theiss design process was initiated. Shawn prayed, made some rough sketches, and then started building a prototype. The new design would be dubbed the *Ferret* as the actual animal counterpart was a sleek, fast, little creature very good at searching out things. Given the task that this aircraft was being designed for, the name fit perfectly. As with former designs, Shawn was confident that the Designer of the Universe was guiding his every move. This craft would indeed fly, and fly well!

Shop wise, things were humming along. In addition to the new *Ferret* design, a variety of small UAV's were being designed, flown, and evaluated. The flying-hamburger-box design of the past had now begun to take on its new shape. The new flying body/bluff body, micro air vehicle, now known as the *TIC* (Tactical Information Craft) design, was quickly moving to the head of the pack (Shawn had chosen not to contact DARPA yet until Theiss Aviation had something in-hand to show them).

The air force "TIC" with extended mobile foot.

Materials were arriving for the completion of the army/CECOM *Tarzan*. Its fuselage was on line with three others. Only having knowledge of the payload weight, Shawn calculated all known factors and ordered a twenty-six horse power engine with alternator and prop. Construction was now underway on craft having twelve-inch wingspans to craft having eighteen-foot wingspans—and everything in-between. Thank you, Lord, money was slowly beginning to roll in.

Within a relatively short period of time, the *Ferret* was completed and ready to be test flown. Winter weather had moved in, and the winds were such that test after test was canceled. In the meantime, the continuing news paper articles were generating yet another demand on the company's officers.

Shawn was little impressed with the request for speaking engagements. On the other hand, Richard enjoyed the opportunity to share the happenings of Theiss Aviation with community clubs, flying clubs, model airplane clubs, church groups, and vocational schools.

The deeper Theiss Aviation became involved with cutting-edge programs, the less that could be presented at the public talks. Then too, there was no way to reveal new designs during show and tell. In time, it was necessary to cut back on such engagements and on visitations to the shop.

There was an evolution of activity going on at Theiss, and its direction was toward everything that had to do with safety and security. Being designers and producers of airframes only was a thing of the past. The in-house integration of avionics, auto pilot systems, and various payloads called for top security measures.

At the time, there were only two doors in the hangar/shop/office complex—an entry door at the southwest side of the building and the hangar door facing east. Both were kept locked at all times. If a person left the building for any reason, the reason was verbally conveyed to another employee along with the expected time of absence. The door was then locked behind the person when they left.

A substantial gate was kept locked at the entry drive during non-production hours. The nearest house to the south side of the runway was the firm's first line of defense. Retired air force Colonel Robert (Bob) Ockerman was a gun licensed guard whose daughter happened to be Theiss Aviation's accountant. For a time, Bob had a German shepherd. He suggested having a sign on the entry gate with a likeness of the dog stating, "I can make it to this gate in 5.2 seconds. How fast are you?"

In addition, an occasional check on the company facility was accomplished by the Pentagon via satellite. Those represented by a certain insurance company weren't the only ones in "good hands!"

A FOOT IN THE DOOR

For Shawn, the old adage, "Be careful about what you pray for, you might get it all!" was surely coming true.

It seemed that all of his contract concerns were coming in—and, at the same time.

The air force contract with Guild Associates was getting very close to its Phase I conclusion and final selection of an aircraft for the development program to be flown. Only two manufacturers remained from the original nine aircraft firms competing for the project—Lockheed Martin and Theiss Aviation.

In Shawn's mind there was a biblical parallel being drawn. In first Samuel (vs.17-32), the young shepherd David dares to take on the giant Goliath in a fight to the death. Christian or not, most people know how the event turned out.

Here in lies the parallel.

Theiss Aviation (the very small David) was face to face with Lockheed Martin (the very large Goliath) in a battle for an air force contract.

To be sure of victory, David prayed—and to be very sure, Shawn and his team were also praying. Only time would tell.

At about this same time, Shawn and Richard were invited to attend a small business seminar in Cleveland, and to display a couple of their craft. During the event, the attention of Orbital Research was drawn (a company based in Cleveland) to the micro air vehicle design the Theiss team was in the final stages of developing—the *TIC* (Tactical Information Craft). Orbital was submitting a proposal to AFRL's munitions directorate at Eglin Air Force Base (in Destin, Florida) for a project that required the development of a small UAV with some very unique capabilities. Might it be what the science firm was in need of for the upcoming Air Force project?

A date was made with Shawn for a show and tell session in Cleveland at the Orbital facility. He showed and told of the virtues of the strange looking *TIC*, and the amazed members of Orbital's staff bought the stubby winged concept—hook, line, and sinker (fuselage, motor, and propeller)!

The project called for the development of a micro air vehicle (MAV) with multiple modes of locomotion; in other words, they wanted a craft that could fly to a designated location, land, then use some form of motion (crawling, hopping, rolling, etc.) to move on the ground. It was also clear that this MAV was anticipated for urban type missions. The *TIC* design (through internal testing by Theiss Aviation) had already proven an uncanny stability in turbulent air, in addition to the ability to fly at speeds of twenty-five miles per hour down to near hover speeds of two miles per hour. This promised to be a great base airframe to build the desired system from.

Orbital won the Phase I project, and soon thereafter the two companies sat down to begin the system design process. After long design meetings between Theiss and Orbital to determine the best form of ground movement, Orbital engineers would be adding a statically balanced foot to the bottom of the craft on which it would be hopping—forward, backward, and possibly up and down stairs. Wow! The air force would have to love a UAV like this!

In the midst of all that Theiss was striving to handle, came two gentlemen from a firm who wanted to develop a new UAV system for a specific need. Dr. John Newport and engineer Phil Gorden presented a deal that Shawn just couldn't turn down.

Strategic Engineering Services would split all costs related to a craft used to fly meteorological equipment for the army.

Shawn had been thinking about designing a plane of a size that would somewhat close the gap between the forty-inch span *Ferret* and the eighteen-foot spanned *Tarzan*. This could be the start of something good. Phone conversations continued between, Shawn, John, and Phil over the next week and a half. Shawn would get to the design just as soon as possible.

Activity in and around the Theiss Aviation firm was definitely on an up-swing as the governmental agency called DARPA was now showing interest in the TIC design.

DARPA had been funding a small MAV (micro air vehicle) development by Aerovironment, but liked the comparison data as presented by the Theiss's tiny *TIC*. They also liked that Theiss was proposing a developmental project in which the small craft could give first responders the ability to fly a small UAV in an urban environment for searching out or detecting harmful chemicals or radiation sources, while the operator was a safe distance away. DARPA was known as the high risk, high payoff agency of the government; if it was on the verge of impossibility to accomplish, DARPA was there.

A good portion of daily prayer was being devoted to the possibility of a DARPA contract. After all, they were the government agency that funded the X-plane contest between Boeing and Lockheed Martin.

Lockheed Martin won that one to the tune of mega billions of dollars. What would they do to little ole Theiss Aviation in the Guild Air Force contest?

Although winters blustery winds were dumping large amounts of snow on the Theiss factory and runways, serious attention was turned to the flight testing of the *Ferret*. If, by the grace of God, Theiss was to win out over Lockheed Martin, then that design had better fly just as it was advertised. On a day that was not as windy or snowy as the majority of days had been, it was decided to try the new sleek design. With test pilot Tom Zets at the controls, Shawn hand-launched the prototype design. Thank heavens Tom was as good of a pilot as anticipated. The craft was indicating a bit of a pitching problem, and very sensitive on the controls.

Regardless, Tom was able to tame the craft enough to get about a twenty-minute flight in before gently landing it in the soft, white snow covering Theiss Field. Realizing the blessing in Tom's abilities to fly, Shawn knew that the design needed to be modified to eliminate the pitching problem and make the craft more stable to fly manually. In the middle of Shawn's design analysis, the call from Nick Dinovo came in.

"Congratulations, the US Air Force has just awarded our team the Phase II contract, and we will be using the Theiss Aviation *Ferret*!"

"Well, how about that?" Shawn was elated.

"In fact," Nick continued, "If Lockheed Martin had won, the air force would have had their planes shipped to Theiss for modification to the program's standards."

The call from Nick concluded with the making of a date for himself and two officers from the Dayton based air force research lab to visit the Theiss facility and see the *Ferret* fly within a couple of days.

One thought prevailed in the minds of Shawn and his VP, "Dear Lord, help us to be ready."

Quickly, the fuselage was cut and lengthened by three inches, and a new wing section built and mounted with added angle of incidence in hopes that the craft would be more stable in flight.

Only one verification flight would be afforded, and it would have to be made early the next morning, for Nick and the officers would be arriving at ten o'clock.

Again, it was Tom Zets at the controls when Shawn launched the craft into the air. Shawn and Richard were praying their way through a very good flight. The modifications had indeed made the craft more docile and brought about the desired flight characteristics as anticipated. All was going great, that is, until just after the landing.

From Richard's vantage point, Shawn had walked over to the craft and seemed to bend low for a closer inspection. The pilot also saw Shawn squat low for a closer look.

In reality, Shawn had leaned over to pick up the plane, but slipped in the snow and fell, knee first onto the trailing edge of the wing. Add to this the dirt embedded in the nose of the craft from landing slightly past the grass of Theiss Field and hitting the plowed dirt ridge in the farmer's field just north of the property line. It was 9:15 a.m., which meant a quick repair had to be made before the 10:00 a.m. arrival of the people who were funding the new project. No problem! Remember, the Theisses were use to last minute repair jobs on aircraft.

The unexpected knock on the shop door caused the three, busy, Theiss personnel to look at their watches, then at one another—9:35 a.m. Good heavens! They were early!

After greeting Nick, Lt. Chris, and Dan Schreider (an air force civilian contractor), Shawn suggested that Richard give the three a quick tour of the office and shop complex. Shawn was actually buying time so as to complete the needed repairs to the damaged *Ferret* before the expected flight demonstration.

As Richard conducted the dog and pony show, he detected the smell of spray paint, an indication that Shawn was finished painting the rehabilitated *Ferret*. The unscheduled tour terminated at the *Ferret's* assembly table.

There she was—a thing of finished beauty! A tribute to the fact that Theiss UAV s were quick to repair (something the air force might well appreciate, but farther down the road).

The following demonstration flights proved the *Ferret* to be true to its purpose.

Pilot Tom Zets knew what they expected to see and he made the craft look effortless to fly as he amazed his Military on lookers. The response to his controls were quick and sure—a plus when the craft was to be flown by an autopilot.

From this point on the Phase II Air Force SUDAMAD project (the lengthy acronym given to the project by AFRL that to this day is still disputed as to what it truly stands for) was a go. The project would initially require three craft to be flown, and they were soon under way, along with a number of *TIC* variations for Orbital's air force project.

In a different section of the shop, the *Tarzan* required for the Lear Siegler / CECOM project was also moving forward and nearing completion. In an attempt to make the craft more rugged for the customer's needs, the design was modified slightly with a new wing design employing a wood spar encased in fiberglass as well as fiberglass skin.

Shawn was spending more and more time at the fiberglass facility located at the Beaver County Airport (site of Shawn's flight activities during his college days) in Beaver, Pennsylvania. It was soon discovered that the small firm retained to produce the fiberglass portions of the wing was overwhelmed with the required process.

After long days at the Theiss shop, Shawn would drive some forty miles in the evening to help lay up the glass wing panels; this in the bitter cold of December.

Unique to the new fiberglass-surfaced wing was its internal fuel tank feature. The center wing section was designed to be a "wet wing," meaning it would carry fuel internally. The five gallon capacity would near double the Tarzan's flight time. The normal five gallon tank could now be moved about within the payload bay area so as to accommodate a variety of odd shaped payloads.

Drawings for the overall dimensions of the anticipated payload were provided to Theiss Aviation so that cardboard models could be made to assure integration into the *Tarzan's* payload area. The payload itself was top, top secret; no one ever spoke of it.

With two AFRL projects, a CECOM project, a meteorological project, and a DARPA White Paper under consideration, it appeared as though Theiss Aviation finally had its foot in the door of government aircraft suppliers.

TIME TO REFLECT

To those in the know, it was easy to see that God's hand had been gently placed on the activities of Theiss Aviation. His hand of preparation had long ago provided for the skills and experiences required to succeed in the high tech areas of unmanned, controlled flight. His hand of guidance and support was ever present in the day to day decisions to be made. It was His hand that opened the doors of opportunity and closed the doors of misjudgment, misunderstanding, misdirection, and mis-intention. By His hand were given those opportunities to share the joy of knowing Jesus with other Christians and Non-Christians alike; these to be found within the governmental agencies of the FAA, CIA, FBI, NASA, and DARPA.

The bond of Christian fellowship was most appreciated when others seemed eager to pray for Theiss Aviation. Many were the prayers offered up in parking lots as the officers of the firm returned from meetings with the army, navy, or air force personnel.

During the first flight activities at Wright Patterson Air Force Base (the SUDAMAD program), the project team of twelve were circled around the *Ferret* UAV praying. Unnoticed was the approach of an air force colonel who inquired as to the group prayer. "We always pray before we fly," chief pilot Tom Zets flatly stated.

The next day, an e-mail was received from the Colonel.

"In my many years as an air force officer, I have witnessed many development programs and various flight teams… few with the degree of proficiency and professionalism displayed by your flight team. And, by the way, I noticed that you know who to go to for the final authority. God bless you!"

Shawn prayed specifically for the opportunity to witness to those that make the decisions in our government, possibly even the president. Although a meeting with that individual has yet to occur, others of noted authority have noticed the Christian life style evident in the young head of the developing aircraft firm.

Often Shawn has been asked why his pricing of Theiss products are so much below other competing companies. It has been stated "Hey! It's the US government. They have plenty of money. Sock it to 'em!"

To this, Shawn replied, "Yes, we do have a lot of paper work, and even some hoops to jump through. However, our size gives us a definite advantage. We don't have the overhead most other firms have. Approach to design and manufacturing is somewhat different, and we don't have a bunch of doctorates to be paid before a program gets off the ground. We make an honest profit, and that's it."

Many were the times when it was felt there was a need for expansion. Praise God that He allowed Theiss to remain very lean so as to keep its pricing as a strong consideration in the minds of procurement agents. "The day will come when US government agencies will realize that their source of money is not from a bottomless pit," Shawn said.

As time went on, it seemed that theory was starting to work. For some time, Theiss Aviation (as a UAV provider) was granted a GSA rating. In fact, they were the first UAV manufacturer to receive the rating for never running over budget or being late for a contract deadline. At the time, both the rating and the company's track record were something that was rare indeed.

For a considerable time, Theiss was the only UAV firm to hold what was believed to be the GSA advantage. As marketed to Shawn, the rating would allow prospective Department of Defense clients to come directly to Theiss Aviation with sole source contracts rather than putting their project needs out to bid for other contractors. Time would unfortunately prove otherwise; the GSA system was cumbersome and not user friendly. Potential clients even informed Shawn that if they had to purchase the Theiss products through GSA, they would buy elsewhere. Hopefully, superior, stable, affordably expendable designs would simply win out over other firm's offerings.

In spite of the time restraints of office, shop, and related travel, there was always time for God's work. Both Shawn and Richard's wives were in the church choir—both were involved in the church school system. Shawn sang and played drums and upright bass with the praise band .

He had helped purchase the drum set for the church using money that had been refunded by UPS for gently destroying an aircraft engine while being shipped to a customer.

Both Shawn and Richard had become one half of a father-son gospel quartet, The Crossroads. Unique to the vocal unit was its on stage musical accompaniment as they sang. Shawn played the upright bass, Brian Wittenmyer was at the piano, and Richard added the mellowness of the muted trombone. Lead vocalist, Dan Wittenmyer, also played electric bass (should Shawn be playing drums).

Often noted was the fact that the double father and son gospel team were also neighbors. Richard often told of his being able to see Shawn's home to his right, Dan's home to the front, and his son Brian's home to his left; all by standing at the front door of the elder Theisses home.

To some, it seemed odd that two men involved in the high tech field of unmanned flight could be found on the platforms of churches singing southern gospel music. To Shawn and his father, it was the opportunity to share the blessings God had provided, both in their business activities and on the road for Jesus.

These were the times that provided the foundation for the strength needed to face the difficult times that lay ahead, and as life on earth would assure—they would come!

WHEN IT RAINS, IT POURS!

February of 2003 had arrived with the force of a lion, and if any lions were around, they were knee deep in snow—that was for sure. The panic that goes with the completion of a project was in evidence as the Leir Siegler/CECOM Tarzan was beginning final assembly.

"Good grief! Don't you guys ever deliver and fly these things in the summer?" The words expressed by paint finisher Dave Koons held serious meaning. It seemed that every one of the largest planes in the Theiss fleet was indeed delivered in the nastiest of winter weather. For this project, it was no different.

Shawn was starting to show signs of fatigue. In order to not miss the target date, he was spending longer and longer days in the shop; very reminiscent of the second NRL order years before. So as to spend some time with her daddy, little Josette was brought to the shop to visit. She even posed smiling in the payload bay of the near finished craft; it was the last of a somewhat lighter moment for the Theiss clan (for some time to come).

On the eighteenth of the month, Hope received a call from Patricia Williams. Bob (the military liaison for Theiss Aviation) had just fallen down stairs at home, seriously cracked his head open, and was on his way to the hospital. Hope called the shop and then headed to the hospital herself. Shawn dispatched his vice president to Bob's side immediately.

Only days before, Bob and Pat had asked Richard to do the eulogy at his funeral. The idea of Bob's pending death from his advancing Lou Gehrig's disease was a most unpleasant thought for Richard. He couldn't help but remember Dick Beck's request for his ashes to be flown over cloud three, this just one week before his death a few years ago.

Could it be that Bob Williams had also had a premonition? Whether he did or not, Bob would not recover from his injuries, and within a few days, he was gone. The Theiss team had lost another member and a dear friend. But as it was in previous situations, there wasn't much time to mourn or reflect. Given the need to be present for Bob's funeral, yet needing to meet the delivery schedule for Lear Siegler, it was decided that Richard would stay behind while Shawn delivered the plane to the East coast. Tom Zets would fly out to meet up with Shawn and complete the acceptance flights.

The plane would first be taken to the facilities of BAI— a company that would be integrating their autopilot system into the *Tarzan* for this contract. As Shawn prepared for the trip, there were still some minor things that needed to be completed on the craft. One such to-do item was to fair in the joints where the wings fold. This, along with a couple other things, would have to be completed at the BAI complex in Easton, Maryland.

As Shawn left the plant, Hope and Richard were concerned that he would be driving at night, having not slept for almost thirty hours. He was determined to be at his destination by eight o'clock on Monday morning. In addition to the lack of sleep and night drive, a snow storm was in the process of dumping snow along most of Shawn's route.

But high winds, bitter cold, heavy snow, and dark of night not withstanding, he made it!

The BAI plant was of good size, clean, and warm; all appreciated by Shawn. Quickly enough, a rapport was established between Shawn and the staff, who themselves were producers of a line of unmanned aircraft.

As Shawn was given a tour of the plant, he remembered that BAI was one of the firms awarded the *Dragon Eye* contract from NRL and the marines. Having been in on the bidding process for *Dragon Eye*, Shawn couldn't help notice a somewhat larger version also being built by the BAI shop. Indeed, it was a slightly larger version and was renamed *Snake Eye*.

After the tour and unloading the *Tarzan* into the BAI facility, it was back into the cold for Shawn; he was on his way to the Philadelphia International Airport (about one hour and forty-five minutes away). Because of the restraints of time, Tom Zets was having to fly to the coast. He would be returning to northeast Ohio in just three days. Much had to be done within the next few days as Tom would be flying both the test and acceptance flights of the *Tarzan* before returning to Ohio.

With Tom acquired, it was back to the BAI facility. As the BAI crew installed the autopilot equipment,

Shawn completed the surface fairings at the wing joints and Tom (also being an A&E) looked the airframe over.

In a matter of hours, the craft was ready for its static engine runs. As the wing fuel tanks were being filled by Shawn and Tom, the worst condition for the moment was in evidence. Fuel was slowly dripping from the trailing edges of the wings.

"Tom!" Shawn half whispered. "We've got a leak!"

Quickly, the fueling stopped and an effort was made to drain what had been pumped into the tank. Although the unexpected does happen, in this case, it couldn't have been at a worse time. To the benefit of Shawn and Tom was their being alone in that section of the shop; no one else knew of the dire situation.

Tom, having knowledge of a sealing compound, went with Shawn in search of the product. They found it at a local airport maintenance shop, poured it into the wing tank and prayed for God's leading.

Answers were forthcoming.

Shawn reasoned, "We can't take a chance on the sealer holding when we run the engine." Tom agreed. "We'll use our standard fuselage tank." Tom agreed.

With the fuselage tank and its plumbing installed, the craft was moved to the engine run-in area. At this point, others joined the Theiss two in a picture perfect series of engine runs.

Picture perfect? Not to Shawn. His mind was remembering the structure of the wing and he was wondering if the leaking fuel had reached the areas of structural foam and had eaten into it. The thought was sickening. He needed to share his thoughts and prayers, but not with Tom.

He found an isolated phone. "Dad, I need you here. How soon can you come?"

"Well," Richard pondered. "Bob's funeral is in the morning, I could take off when I finish my part. What do I need to bring?" Richard asked.

"Just you! We have what we need here. Give me a call when you get close, and I'll talk you in." Although Richard was a bit confused, he concluded with, "Love you! I'll call when I get close."

"What on earth could be happening out there? Guess I'll know soon enough." Richard reasoned.

Col. Bob Williams was having a funeral befitting the hero he was—dressed in his military uniform and with full military guard and honors. Many from far and wide were in attendance. His widow, Patricia, had done well.

Richard's eulogy was not easy to do, his heart went out to Pat, seated only a few feet away, just days out of the hospital herself from brain surgery.

She and Bob were so instrumental in working with the military, and now he would never know that Richard would be rushing off to help with a delivery to the naval air station at Lakehurst, New Jersey.

His part finished, Richard kissed the company officer (and most able wife, Hope) goodbye, and quietly left the funeral parlor.

His trip to the east coast was horrendous. Having no load in his pickup truck, it was not doing well with the heavy snow fall through the Pennsylvania mountains. Then, to top it all off, he became lost somewhere in Maryland, at night.

But despite the slight detour, he finally made it, much to the relief of both he and Shawn. As Shawn updated Richard on the situation and shared his concerns, both Theiss Aviation officers turned the entire situation over to the only one in complete control—God.

Now it was for the two earthlings to exercise complete faith (still being of human capacity). They needed spiritual help.

It was Saturday and the day for the test flight had arrived. The Tarzan had been transferred to a private air strip on a private island a few miles off of the Atlantic Ocean shoreline.

The Island was owned by the BAI president, Richard Bernstien. As Richard Theiss was being given a tour of the Island's fabulous home site by its owner, Shawn, Tom, and the BAI crew were preparing the *Tarzan* and its ground station for flight. As the two Richards joined the flight crew, an evident test-flight-tension was in the air. Not to mention that the air itself was frigidly miserable.

With a temperature below freezing, the unhampered, off-ocean wind yielded a wind-chill factor that seemed unreal. For Shawn and BAI manager, Kirk, who were both restraining the plane during the engine warm up, the cold, prop wash was mind numbing. Then, Shawn started the long walk with the plane to the far end of the runway (The *Tarzan* did not have brakes installed).

For this first test flight, Tom would be having a co-pilot on what was called a buddy box. The twin transmitters would allow both pilots access to flight control, and control could be switched between the pilots by the ground control station operator.

The co-pilot was one of BAI's test pilots. It was felt that the BAI pilot might have to fly the demonstration and acceptance flight should Tom Zets not be available. Given the tight time schedule, Tom would fly the craft first, get it trimmed out, then (if all was performing as expected) would hand the control over the BAI pilot to train him a little.

All were ready as Kirk gave the signal for Shawn to release for take-off. The engine roared to full power and Shawn through both arms up to indicate the start of the take-off roll. Dick Bernstien, camcorder in hand, was filming the fast approaching UAV.

Moments later, Theiss Aviation team members heaved a sigh of relief as they watched the lift-off response to Tom's control input. The *Tarzan* was climbing and flying into the clear blue sky above!

Kirk could be heard calling out the flight control data from his position at the ground control station console. "Air speed 55 mph, altitude 500 feet."

After trimming the craft manually, the team began making adjustments to the autopilot system. When engaged, the BAI autopilot system proved to work well.

Kirk now called out the total flight time and, with Shawn's approval, suggested the plane be brought in for a landing so that it could be given a thorough check over. It was then suggested that since all was performing well, maybe the BAI pilot should have just a little time to fly the craft in the pattern before

Tom brought the *Tarzan* back to land. The flight team agreed, and preparations were quickly made to do so. The BAI pilot visually acquired the trim settings on Tom's control box and made the same adjustments to the co-pilot box (this would assure that the craft continued to fly as trimmed when switched over to the co-pilot box).

When all were ready, pilot Tom indicated that he was turning control over to the copilot. With that statement, Kirk flipped the switch on the ground control station that gave control to the co-pilot box and the BAI pilot. In the next few moments, the shock of disbelief was felt by all present. The big roaring engine stopped.

Chaos almost controlled the situation as for a few seconds, Tom and the BAI pilot bantered as to who was going to quickly land the bird. Shawn quickly barked out "Tom, do you have this?"

"Yes, I have this!" was Tom's reply.

"Give the controls back to Tom!" Shawn called out to Kirk.

With that, Tom now found that he had the control of a heavy, hot glider, with not much altitude, over the Atlantic Ocean. As a reminder, this was the first time Tom had ever flown this plane. Again, being children of God, the petitions for his help were automatic for the Theiss team.

For the BAI crew, it was amazing to see Tom bring the craft, dead stick, back over the end of the narrow runway. As it had to be, the approach was fast, but the landing was hard. The nose gear folded back under the stress, which took away any ability for Tom to steer the craft on the ground. Then, the crosswind tracked the plane to the left just enough to drop the left main gear off the hard surface and into the grass. Once snagged, the craft tracked completely off the runway, and ground to a stop in the rough, frozen turf.

The silence was deafening for a few seconds. Disbelief of the moment was apparent in all present. Tom felt so bad that he put the pilot box down, and took a walk down the runway to clear his mind. Shawn joined him and assured Tom that this was in no way his fault and thanked him for the incredible job of bringing the bird back in one piece!

With clear minds, Tom and Shawn both returned to the site to assess what needed to be done next. Damage was limited to the nose gear, cowl, and prop. All on board equipment was undisturbed (a tribute to the craft's design and construction), and the rest of the airframe appeared to be undamaged.

The question was, what caused the engine to stop?

Leading the charge to find an answer was first pilot, Tom Zets. After all, he seemed to be in control at the time of the incident. Tom began to look over cable connections at the ground control station and switch settings. He then turned his attention to the pilot and co-pilot boxes to check their switch settings. All appeared to be set correctly, with the exception of one switch on the co-pilot box— the engine run switch was in the off position. If the switch had been in that position when control was switched from the pilot box to the co-pilot box, the autopilot system would have instantly seen an engine off command and killed the engine.

Tom informed the team of his findings. In retrospect, the scenario made complete sense; Tom has control, control is given to the BAI pilot, engine quits. For some reason, the BAI pilot would not confirm the possibility that he had neglected to check the engine run switch before control was given to him. This made for a very tense situation, but carried no weight without the BAI pilot admitting to any wrong-doing. Tom was being left out to dry, or hang, as the case may be. As might be expected, he was looking for justification.

BAI's president, Richard Berenstine, and superintendent Kirk were both looking to their pilot for an admission to at least the possibility of his transmitter's engine run switch being off at a time when it should have been on. None was forthcoming.

Welcome was Shawn's statement, "Let's get back to the shop and get things ready to fly on Monday." Representatives from both Lear Siegler and the US Army (CECOM) would arrive early Monday morning, expecting to see a demonstration and acceptance flight. For the moment, a new subject was activated.

Two hours later, Shawn assigned work to be accomplished. Richard would handle rebuilding the engine cowling. Shawn would himself get a new propeller, fix the nose gear, and add a trim tab to the left wing. The latter adjustment was the result of conversation with pilot Tom Zets. Tom would be assisting where needed.

Long hours later, the craft was ready to once again prove its flight ability. But this time it would have to be with the BAI pilot in full control; Tom would be flying back to Ohio Sunday evening. This would be the first time that the BAI pilot had actually been at the controls of the *Tarzan*, and it would have to happen in front of the clients.

Understandably, the Theiss Team was more than a bit on edge. Just before leaving, Tom expressed deep disappointment that the truth of the former situation had not been resolved. Richard assured him that all involved knew the truth of the matter and that God would indeed set things straight. And, so He did.

Monday morning came. Even though the motel room was fairly sound proof, it was evident to Shawn and Richard upon awakening that the weather outside was horrendous. The TV news told of winds in excess of thirty miles per hour and it was snowing to the point of a white out. Richard, who was a lover of winter snows, had never appreciated it more. There would be no demonstration and acceptance flight that day. No placing the Theiss *Tarzan* into the control of the BAI pilot. No reason but to praise the Lord for His goodness.

The Lear Siegler and Army clients were treated to a long walk around and talk about the *Tarzan*, and were even shown a flight video of the craft filmed just days before (less the hard landing, of course). The clients understood the need to cancel flights that day, and agreed to push the acceptance and training flights back a little. They also agreed to allowing the acceptance flight to be made at the Lakehurst, New Jersey naval airbase—the same location where the scheduled pilot training would occur. BAI seemed most happy to help ship the Theiss craft to its new home.

Within a couple month's time, Shawn had ground schooled, and Tom had flight trained the Lear Siegler pilots to handle the Tarzan. Theiss products were now on both the east and west coasts of the United States.

The entire program from start to finish had been anything but pleasant. In fact, Shawn began to think seriously about discontinuing the Tarzan line due to the intense labor and stress levels that were required to build them. For the remaining months of 2003 and most of 2004, Theiss Aviation focused on the ongoing AFRL projects with Guild and Orbital. All things considered, the Tarzan line would have become extinct had not an engineering firm (Kalscott) out of Topeka, Kansas, ordered three more. The intent to order came shortly before Christmas, and the prospective money to be made was something that Shawn, reluctantly, could not pass up.

Kalscott had obtained an army contract to fly a variety of payloads for testing. The three new craft were to be modified to have no bottoms in the forward payload sections. Kalscott would provide a frame or tray-like structure that would contain different payloads for platform testing. These trays required numerous bolt holes to be perfectly positioned on the inside of the fuselage payload area walls. Now, the craft that was laborsome to build had just become even more so.

As work on the three began that winter, shop floor space diminished. Sub-assemblies soon occupied three of the six large table tops. Smaller craft and the company officers shared what little space was left. Shawn went to the drawing board and quickly produced plans for additions to the main shop and office areas.

Shortly, the original building construction crews were back working at the Theiss facility. Shawn's office, a reception area with kitchenette, Richard's office, an engineering office, and a conference room were starting to take shape. As with most other company oriented construction, the work was being accomplished in the dead of winter. Cold mud seemed to be everywhere.

At least the company seemed to be going forward. Only time would tell.

STRETCHED THIN

The spring of 2005 was fast approaching and so was a commitment Shawn had made some months earlier.

Every two years, the US Department of Homeland Defense hosts a gathering of innovators and producers of anything and everything that can be used for homeland security. The event is affectionately known as FPED (Force Protection Equipment Demonstration), and is by invitation only for both vendors and visitors. Theiss Aviation had received an invitation to attend and display their products, and being that there was no charge to do so, Shawn felt that this could be a good opportunity to expand the company clientele base. As in previous years, the three day event would be located at the Quantico Marine Base just south of Washington, D.C.

Shawn's original plan was to take and demonstrate one of each of the company's four major lines of UAV craft. But as the show drew closer, things were not shaping up for a Theiss Aviation participation. It would be impossible to have a Tarzan demonstrator ready for flight by the program's date. Then too, demonstration pilot Tom Zets would be flying elsewhere at that time, so there would be no one present to fly the demonstrations. "No," flatly stated Shawn, "I'll simply have to call and cancel."

Easier said than done. The FPED coordinator promptly called Shawn and expressed a mixture of unhappy thoughts and gentle threats over the "no-show" decision. The program had already been printed showing Theiss Aviation as one of only two flight demonstration teams. The other was the US Air Force (not bad company to keep). As the call continued, the attitude turned to virtual begging from the coordinator for Theiss Aviation to attend. The lengthy phone conversation ended on an amiable note with Shawn agreeing to reconsider. Eventually, Shawn and Jim Suarez would become the closest of friends.

The Kalscott Engineering *Tarzan* nearest to completion would be taken to Quantico. The likelihood of it being ready to fly by then was in doubt. Time was too short for the proper engine installation and flight tests to be performed. Shawn would have to fly both the *Ferret* and *Super Ferret*. The smaller *TIC* demonstrations would depend on the prevailing winds. It must be understood that Shawn had only flown the *Ferret* prototype once, and the *TIC* only a few times—his R/C piloting experience was minimal at best.

Currently the *Super Ferret* was in the autopilot tuning process for the Strategic Engineering project. One of the two partners in Strategic, Phil Gordon, would join Shawn and Richard at Quantico for FPED. He would help man the Theiss display area and program the *Super Ferret's* autopilot system for the flight demonstrations.

The Sunday evening's departure for the Quantico marine base was rather usual. Although spring was at hand, a late season snow was laying up deep inches of the cold white stuff. Shawn was spending much time on his belly and back while securing the variety of aircraft and show items to the inside of a small U-Haul trailer (Theiss Aviation still had its larger trailer, but was currently without a vehicle to pull it).

Of course, the loading activity was taking much longer than planned. When the packing process was completed, it was early the next morning (about 2:30 a.m.). As Shawn and his VP finally settled into the tow truck, they were startled by bright lights just mere feet from the front of their vehicle. Then they heard someone order them to step out of the cab.

"Hands up!"

It was only then that they recognized their neighbor and self appointed security man, Bob Ockerman, who had been watching someone taking lots of items from the shop and was not going to let them get out of the driveway with it (the heavy snow fall had blurred the identity of the culprits). On the other hand, the two Theisses never saw or heard the approach of Bob in his snow white auto (with lights off).

Things set straight, the sojourn continued toward the Washington, D.C. area. The all night, snow-hampered trip, finally concluded at the gates of the Quantico marine base, which was no easy place to access.

A day had been allowed for the set-up of the displays. It was soon evident that Theiss Aviation was located in what would prove to be a very noisy area; loud speakers and warning systems companies were on all sides.

As the week moved on things became rather routine. The by-invitation-only crowds were small, but very impressive. And they seemed to be very interested in what Theiss had to offer.

International statesmen, the secretaries of the army, navy, and air force (along with their staff members), generals, admirals, and of course, the secretary of homeland defense; blue bloods all.

As expected, security was very tight. President Bush used the base in most of his travels, and every precaution was taken for his safety. Each day, Shawn was reminded (at the pilots meeting) that should he fly out of the designated demonstration area, he would be shot down.

Although the winds were high each day, Shawn was able to complete the entire week's flight demonstrations without having one plane shot out of the air. He was also able to fly each craft (except the Kalscott *Tarzan*, which thankfully was not finished) without incident or indication of the fact that the company owner had never flown the *Super Ferret* previously, and had very little experience in flying the other two craft. God's hand was undeniable to the Theiss Team.

Launching the Super Ferret at FPED.

The real bonus for the week's effort came in the form of Christians and Christian firms in the industry being revealed to the Theiss Company.

The next door display booth was occupied by the representatives of Carolina Unmanned Vehicles. Being bonafied born again Christians, a bond between the two firms was established that would prove to be fruitful both faith-wise and business-wise to the day of this writing.

The manner in which God chooses to reveal one Christian to another is a source of constant amazement.

Because of security, only one video firm was approved to record the events of FPED. A single videographer and the owner/director of the firm accompanied the Theiss Team to the flight line each day. It was most evident that both men were very proficient at their profession.

On the first day of flight demonstration activity, the owner of the video firm (a man in his mid-sixties) asked Richard, "If I were to mention the Emmaus Walk, would it have any meaning to you?"

The Emmaus Walk is a Methodist ministry whereby men and women of all Christian faiths meet for a three day weekend to petition the presence of Jesus Christ and to walk with them as He did with the disciples shortly after His resurrection on the day that was to become Easter Sunday.

Just a few years earlier, Richard Theiss had been part of an Emmaus Walk weekend and could certainly attest to the excitement being displayed by his new-found Christian friend.

Out of the hundreds in attendance at FPED, the posed question had been asked of probably the only other person there having a knowledge and understanding of that experience.

Indeed, the presence of God's people could be found in all endeavors of life, even from among the high-tech world of self proclaimed achievers who were working for, and in concert with, the United States Department of Defense. The most apparent result of being a part of the FPED program was that other firms were interested in partnering with Theiss Aviation.

The ride home from the show was full of recollection of the week's events, and conversations of the possible teaming strategies that could benefit Theiss Aviation. The following summer months were sprinkled with various phone conversations and proposal writing along with continued UAV fabrication.

It was fall when Shawn received an unexpected call from Kalscott Engineering. The firm that ordered the three *Tarzans* was being cut back (contract dollar wise) and really could now afford only one. All three of the craft were near completion and were hogging much of the shop's floor space.

Basic to the resulting negotiations was Shawn's understanding of the problem. He could remember all too well when the naval research lab had cancelled four of the Tarzans as the result of President Clinton's cutback of military funding. However, despite his sympathetic understanding of the problem, Shawn could not simply absorb the material and labor costs that had been incurred in producing the three big birds. The contract was discussed and negotiations made between Theiss and Kalscott. Here again, the hand of God could be seen in the final rework of the original contract.

Within a few weeks, Kalscott dispatched a truck to pick up their single, now expensive, craft. The remaining two (still taking up much needed floor space) were now the property of Theiss Aviation. Winners all. Well... almost.

After signing all new contract documents and receiving the balance of payment due, the Theiss Team loaded the Tarzan airframe into the Kalscott truck. The craft was strapped down, the truck door closed, handshaking completed, and the Kalscott representative was in the driver seat ready to head back west. Being winter once again (the time that *Tarzans* were usually shipped) the Theiss Airfield was dressed in a few inches of white snow—very pretty, very soft, and very slippery. As the Kalscott truck (with *Tarzan* onboard) started to move off of the tarmac at the rear of the hangar, it soon became bogged down.

Shawn fired up the company tractor and attempted to assist the truck out of the deepening ruts. Having gone through a lengthy effort to advance only some fifty feet, it was decided to call for a wrecker to try and pull the Kalscott truck back onto the driveway. The wrecker (with truck in tow) was good for almost another seventy-five feet before it too became bogged down. What now? Of course, what else? Another really big wrecker did well for another 150 feet, before it too joined a pretty impressive parade of stuck trucks!

If not for the comical situation, stress levels would have been very high. Only after winching itself back onto the entry drive, did the really big wrecker do the job (as hoped for) and pull the rest of the parade to solid ground—three hours later.

The deep, long ruts in the normally smooth, grassy field, long served Shawn as a reminder of the additional cost of the whole fiasco, all on Theiss Aviation's dime. Live and learn!

FAST FORWARD

Over the next few months, it became evident that Theiss Aviation was being locked into a certain segment of the government's procurement process. When Shawn established Theiss Aviation, his business card touted "Essence of the Past in Products of the Present." After becoming a manufacturer of UAV's only his cards stated, "Experienced Leaders in Innovative Aircraft Design." As with most production companies, Theiss too hoped to obtain large quantity production contracts.

After having been involved with over a dozen contracts at this point, it seemed that the Department of Defense research facilities (AFRL, NRL, etc.) were very much interested in the firm's ability to satisfy specific needs (design wise). And so, the company (more often than not) was engaged in the earliest of a three-phase procurement system.

Phase I dealt with the design and basic development of a new design that should, could, and would satisfy the client's needs and desires. The Theiss design team (Shawn plus one) were at all times aware that creative design and development came from God, not them. Their part in the equation was to ask (pray), expect answers (have faith), and then look and listen (receive). Although, admittedly, this approach to standard engineering practice is a bit strange (to most), it is responsible for yielding craft that carry more weight than ever believed possible, at speeds faster or slower than thought possible, and with a power setting thought to be impossible. With God, *all* things are possible!

Phase II dealt with an exercise called "Proof of Concept." This is where Theiss Aviation really stands apart from other firms. For the smaller craft, the government's expected months of time required to build and fly a prototype (first craft) is often reduced to days or at most weeks to be ready for flight. From that point in time, it is flight tested and fine tuned. Mission development can then require a year or so depending on the program's goals and complexity.

To date, Theiss Aviation has obtained and excelled in both Phase I and Phase II portions of various projects. Now, for Theiss Aviation, comes the illusive Phase III. This Phase is where a design moves from Prototype status to limited production status. This is the Phase that can catapult a design into the realm of high volume production orders.

For Theiss Aviation, small numbers of their designs are required from time to time. However, the only craft to require an assembly line has been and continues to be the largest, most laborsome and space-taking *Tarzan*. For the present, it's Phase I and II projects that pay the bills.

Flashback, as our nation continued to deal with the problems of terrorism (at home and abroad), the bi-annual involvement with the FPED program became more fruitful. The second FPED attendance led to demonstrations being flown for the FBI at their Quantico home base location, and eventually their purchase of a *TIC* system. Prior to attending the third FPED event, Shawn received a call from one of the program's coordinators. The lady told Shawn that she had been reviewing photos of the craft that Theiss Aviation would be showing in a few weeks, and one flying shot was of a large bird.

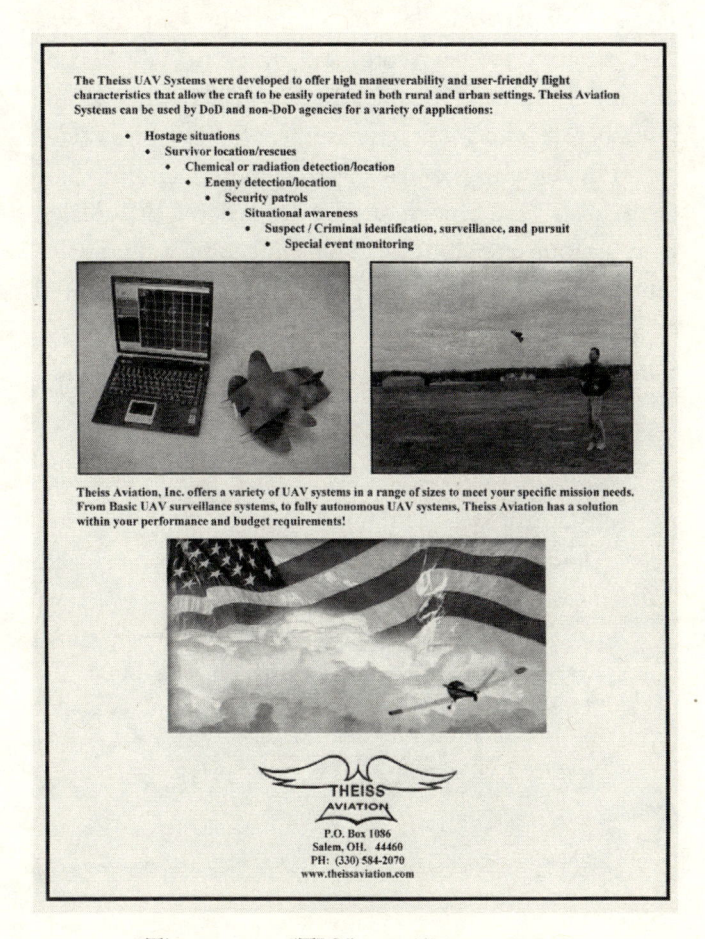

The compact "TIC" surveillance system.

"Did you intend to send this photo?" asked the coordinator.

"Yes!" was Shawn's reply.

"You're bringing a bird?" She asked.

"Yes we are."

The flying thing in question was a six-foot spanned *Vulture*. Shawn had designed it to represent the type that is native to every continent on earth. While conducting flight tests for the air force in Dayton a couple years before, the Theiss Team observed live birds (vultures) flying with the black *Ferret* when in circling patterns. This gave Shawn an idea for a new UAV design with unique capabilities. The concept would evolve into a line of craft called NIRVs, or nature inspired reconnaissance vehicles.

Theiss Aviation's Vulture NIRV.

When deployed, the *Vulture* is generally joined by a few more actual vultures (hoping to get in on the tasty morsel spotted by the Theiss Aviation decoy)— a perfect setting for the mission of surveillance. This hiding among the real birds would be dubbed by Theiss Aviation as "natural masking." Depending on wind and thermal conditions, the *Vulture* can stay aloft for extended periods of time at little to no power settings.

The response of the FPED attendees to the big bird suspended from above was most gratifying. Adding to its realism was its power source; an internally mounted electric ducted fan unit. A bonus for both the Theiss firm and the interested were two smaller NIRVs to either side of the *Vulture*. The *Hawk* was great at moving flocks of birds off of active runways, and the *Seagull* opened another setting for sea and seashore surveillance. All in all, the time required for the internally funded design and development of the Theiss flock of fine feathered friends seemed worth the dime spent (something to be appreciated by Hope, the company's money manager). Very soon, it would prove to be even more worthwhile!

Within a few weeks, Shawn got a call from the air force research laboratory at Wright Patterson Air Force Base. The question posed was how soon might he, Shawn, be able to meet with the staff concerning a program that most probably would involve the smaller of the bird designs? A date was set. The meeting held in Dayton exposed an urgent need for meeting a long standing requirement for covert surveillance capabilities. The Theiss birds were heading in the right direction. They had the appearance of nature while flying overhead (even other birds seemed to feel so). So far, a good start.

"Now," the officers asked, "Can you have them fold their wings after they land?"

Not being one to pass up a good challenge, Shawn answered in the affirmative, "I'm sure that we can!" So far, so good. Then came the biggie.

"Shawn, we're under the gun on this one," the chief investigator flatly stated. "We would need something in hand within a few months time. Is it possible?"

The reply was firm and confident, "I'm sure it is!"

This, as it turned out, was just what the air force team wanted to hear. To prove that point, money was arranged for up front and was paid up front—something welcomed by the firm's treasurer.

Once again there would be enough green to keep the doors open—ever blessed, ever appreciated!

OPEN DOORS—
CLOSED DOORS

The walk of the Christian is made up of both open and closed doors. Though it may not be initially apparent, in time, he sees benefit in both.

In 2007, NASA (National Air and Space Administration) petitioned Shawn to be a part of a pending five-year lease program. A few, from among the American producers of unmanned aircraft, would be selected to provide UAV systems and pilots on an as needed basis in support of the NASA Earth Sciences Program. Shawn signed on. For the next year, the Theiss firm was made to jump through a never ending succession of hoops including inspections, the listing of every item contained within the walls of the shop, and numerous letters and conference calls.

Then came the welcomed, "Congratulations!" Theiss Aviation had earned one of ten NASA lease contracts. Now, maybe the two eighteen-foot wing spanned *Tarzans* left over from the Kalscott contract will have found a home. Door open? No, door closed... at least for now. No actual work has come from that contract to date.

But in 2009, another door opened. A contract firm dealing with the navy's weapons development branch, NAVAIR, was looking into the possibility of the Theiss

Tarzan satisfying an unspecified navy need. The firm's name was Brandes Associates, Inc. (or BAI—not to be confused with Bernstein Aerospace, Inc. with whom Theiss had previous business).

Whoa! "Could the navy maybe use two of the aircraft?" Shawn inquired.

The answer was yes. As a matter of fact, they would require two.

Could there be a problem with finally having a contract on the two big birds occupying so much of the needed floor space? Yes. How about two big ones? First, the planes would have to be completed with avionics, engine installation, autopilot systems, and, oh yes, throw in a trailer that would contain both craft and a complete ground control station. All this with an unbelievably short amount of time in which to deliver the contract.

The second glitch was the need for some $80,000 to purchase the engines, props, and pretty much everything except the already finished airframes. A visit to the bank should do it.

Perhaps this would be a good place to mention the State of the Union;— not according to the president (who currently happened to be one Barack Hussein Obama), but rather as recorded by those less corrupt and liberal within the media (slim pickins indeed).

In just the short period of two years, this elected individual along with an internal staff of dedicated, devious supporters have overtaken every major player in industry, commerce, energy, health, education, Wall Street, and the banks. Housing and food will bring the resisters of the administration's agenda in line soon enough. How do we know this? The Bible tells us so.

As Shawn entered the early stages of contract development, it soon became evident that he and the members of the Theiss firm were living in the most interesting of times. Some were calling it difficult times. Others referred to it as drastic times. The Bible calls it "The End Times."

In current times, the US Congress has been pumping billions of dollars into the banking system with the prediction that they, the banks, in turn would lend small businesses their needed funding to survive—not so!

The bank with which Theiss Aviation had been since its founding some twenty years past, said no. Two other banks said no. The business plan Shawn had presented to the banks contained the stipulation of the firm paying off all indebtedness (something God desires of all who love and look to his Son for the fulfillment of their needs).

As the contract between Theiss Aviation and Brandes (BAI) was drawing close to completion, Shawn was sensing tremendous pressure. How could he sign the document without the funds to complete the two craft, design and build the ground station trailer, arrange for the testing of the planes, and set out the training schedule for the BAI pilots? He couldn't, but God could. Now what? Pray of course!

The answer was received. Within the family of God is the family of Theiss, and within the family of Theiss is the family of Groves, and within the family of Groves is sister Michelle. Would it be possible? Would she consider a loan of this magnitude? Who might she and husband Roger turn to? God, of course!

With God's plan in motion, Shawn initiated the contract and soon received a purchase order for two turn-key *Tarzans* with a complete ground station. Praise Him!

Hectic might well describe the next few months' activities at Theiss Aviation, Inc. Oh! The installation of essentials seemed to be going well enough, as long as the essentials were on hand. The engine company was providing reasons for the delay of both engines (which was a bit puzzling); could they too be dealing with the resistant banks? Shawn tried to understand. In addition, there were delays in receiving the autopilot systems.

Weeks passed, still no engines or autopilots. How could work proceed on the engine mounts with no engines? And how can the flight control system be installed and tested without the autopilots?

BAI called. It had been requested that the planes have navigation lights. At this stage of the game, the installation of the needed wiring would be no easy task.

Two very knowledgeable builders and R/C pilots were brought on board to help carry the load of completing the aircraft. Both Rich Evans and Al (Butch) Myers would be charged with onboard electronics and the final construction of all wire harnesses. In addition, Rich Evans would be receiving *Tarzan* flight instruction from Tom Zets so as to later become one of the Theiss pilots who would be training the BAI pilots.

With only two weeks left until the shipping deadline, one engine was received as time was becoming very critical. Now the welder could do his thing on the engine mounts. At this date, the realistic concern was if there would be time for the proper testing of the craft before shipping them to the California destination. Shawn made a call to the BAI agent requesting an additional week so as to verify all systems before shipment. The delayed answer came—negative!

The shipment in itself was a nightmare. A lowboy tractor trailer unit was retained by Shawn for the trip from North Benton, Ohio to Camp Roberts, California. One plane would be wood braced (two-by-fours) on the inside of the ground station command trailer. The second plane would be completely encased within its own plywood box. In turn, the plywood box would then be strapped onto the forward section of the lowboy trailer.

The second engine arrived just a few short days before the scheduled shipment. However, the autopilots wouldn't arrive until the day before system shipment.

Word had reached Shawn that a flight program scheduled to fly the week after BAI's reserved week for flying (at the Camp Roberts Air Strip) had been cancelled. He quickly placed a call. Might it be possible that BAI could have their time slot slipped back one week to complete and test fly the craft? The BAI agent seemed adamant—Theiss would have to meet the original contract deadline.

Hours were being added to the scheduled work day. Both Shawn's wife, Charlene, and Richard worked late nights sizing and cutting lumber and plywood for the boxing and bracing of the planes while in transit. Shawn continued to install as much of the final components as possible in both aircraft.

As Christian brothers volunteered to help load the lowboy tractor trailer standing by, it became only too clear; Theiss Aviation would be shipping aircraft that had not been ground or flight tested. In fact, the autopilots were still in their original shipping boxes as received by Theiss Aviation.

While Shawn and Richard watched the truck pull away, the physical and mental exhaustion started to set in. Shawn had been working seventy hours without a break. The next few hours would be devoted to packing his suitcase for the early morning flight to California. Maybe he could get some rest on the plane.

Within a few days, Shawn and the near total of his project offerings to BAI and NAVAIR were assembled at the Camp Roberts Air Strip (near total because a few items were still being received at the shop for re-shipment to the California test site). Test and acceptance flight pilot Tom would be joining Shawn and second pilot, Rich Evans, on Wednesday of the very busy week.

As the designated time for the actual test flights drew near, so did unforeseen problems that had been lurking behind the rushed delivery schedule. A misconnect in the alternator wiring blew the ignition system of the first engine started. The required rewiring of the system would surely cause a costly time delay, but was inevitable. The team went to work removing the damaged components. The engine manufacturer was contacted, and the replacement parts were ordered. Unfortunately, the timing could not have been worse, for by the time the situation was assessed and parts were ordered, it was late in the day on Friday. This meant that the new parts were now four days out from being delivered to the anxious Theiss team; four days of no testing progress.

Finally, the new parts arrived early the following week and were promptly installed. This time, the Theiss team took extra precaution in assuring everything was wired correctly. Shawn and the team moved on.

With the ignition system correctly installed, the initial engine runs seemed to go flawlessly; then, another speed bump. Post engine run inspections revealed that a hair-line crack had developed in one of the engine mount arms. Shawn was not willing or able to invest the time required to pull the engine and ship it back to the manufacturer for the mounting arm issue to be addressed. No, he would have to pull the engine, find a local off-base welder, and fix it himself.

Within 24 hours, the repair had been made. While remounting the first plane's repaired engine mount, the second plane was readied for engine runs. Shawn could not believe his eyes as he inspected the plane after the initial engine run-up, and discovered that it too had developed a hair-line crack in the same location as aircraft number one. How could this be?

At this point, Shawn made two phone calls; First was to the "Keeper of the Green"… Mom Theiss! "Send money!" was the underlying cry.

Second, Shawn made a call to the engine manufacturer. "Shawn," the engine man flatly stated, "we've never had this problem before."

Engines were shipped overnight back to their manufacturer, returned and reinstalled, restarted and re-cracked at the weld again. Time delay!

As a desperate move, Shawn designed an aluminum plate to fit behind the engine mountings and had them machined at an off-base location. Time delay!

Time was not the only item running short. The new wiring, pulling and re-mounting of the engines, welding and machining of metal parts, two UAV pilots (who come at a very high price) standing around with nothing to fly—it was all costing Theiss Aviation thousands!

By weeks' end, Tom Zets had run out of time and was on his way back to Ohio, never having flown either of the planes. Now Shawn found himself with less than a day to test fly the planes with a pilot who had never flown the craft before.

Without question, Rich Evans was a fine R/C pilot. To top it off he had the experience of flying very large model planes; a dozen or so near the size of the Theiss *Tarzan* were in his work shop back in Ohio. However, a UAV of any size is a bird of a different feather. Models are built as light as possible and usually have power to spare. UAVs on the other hand are built as strong as possible so that they can carry substantial loads at required speeds and are typically underpowered.

One can only surmise what was in Rich's mind as he contemplated the pending flight. As was planned, he would have had plenty of time in the air and on the ground by now. But, the hectic activities of the past week left him with an empty bag.

As might have been expected, prior to this moment, Shawn, Rich, and the ground control operator had joined in prayer. God was in control.

One of the BAI pilots who was to have had training over the past week was standing by with a camcorder for recording the flight. Shawn walked the plane to the far end of the runway and waited for Rich to gun the engine. Rich did and the plane roared down the runway, then lifted quickly into the blue California sky.

As recorded, the craft handled well for some thirty minutes, but was intermittently loosing communication with the ground control station. The loss was brief when it happened, but enough to be a little unnerving. As always, what goes up (at some time) must come down. Again, Rich Evans might have been thinking, "This baby is going to be a bundle to handle."

Shawn inquired as to Rich being comfortable with the landing; Rich was visibly struggling with the big bird and gentle flight patterns. Before getting a commitment from the pilot, the ground control tech asked if Shawn might want for him to bring the plane in. Coincidentally, the tech was a large scale R/C pilot, but also had UAV experience. Wisely, Rich took the technician up on his offer. Now, Shawn replaced the ground control operator in the trailer as the pilot control box changed hands.

As the new pilot began to set up on approach for landing, the intermittent communications glitch became more prominent. This led to moments of calmness, followed by seconds of terror. The plane would be flying as desired one minute, then would begin to wander for a couple seconds until the communications glitch passed, all the while the *Tarzan* was getting closer and closer to the ground. As the *Tarzan* crossed over the end of the runway, one final glitch caused it to drift off to the side of the hard top.

The rough sod beside the landing strip snagged the main gears, causing it to settle onto the unimproved surface. The nose wheel then dug into the soft dirt and the plane up-ended nose first, bending the nose gear back and breaking the prop and one of the exhaust stacks. Inspection determined no other damage, and the plane would be flight ready again within a few days. However, the clock had run out on this first attempt to get the system tested and delivered to the client.

Shawn's return to Ohio was clouded with much uncertainty, and much more indebtedness. Time again for the will of God to be realized. If the current situation was another closed door, it was a gigantic door that could conceivably close down Theiss Aviation once and for all. The thought was sickening and was sensed by all of the key members of the firm. The present situation being what it was, all concerned were crying out for reasons—anything that could explain the delays and malfunctions. Anything!

THE LAST DAYS

Considering worldwide events and the out of control direction our own nation is heading, one has only to conclude that we are living in what the Bible has declared to be "The Last Days" or "The End of Times." But for whom?

The final chapters in God's word, the Book of Revelation, reveal that what can be seen on earth—increased earthquakes, hurricanes, tornadoes, floods, and lawlessness earth-wide—are only indications of the wars going on in the unseen realm of the spirit world.

With this in mind, could Satanic forces not want for the US Navy (NAVAIR) to benefit from the use of the already proven Theiss *Tarzan*? Could the amount of the contract, being such that Theiss Aviation would finally become free of indebtedness anger the dark angels to the point of disruption? Then too, considering that Shawn and his staff look to God and his Son Jesus for the solution to all of their needs, might not one conclude that Theiss Aviation was the target of demonic activity?

The contracting firm's agent assured Shawn that he would do everything possible to continue the contract, but the final decision would be in the hands of the navy. Shortly thereafter, Shawn received word from the navy. If time was an issue, why didn't Theiss request an extension for the proper testing of the craft in question?

Shawn quickly sent his response giving the two dates for his requests, the person to whom they were given, and the negative response to both requests received.

At this point, Shawn, Richard, and Hope reasoned that the navy seemed open to considering answers to the problems that plagued the week of test activities. Their prayers were for someone in command to realize that the problems experienced were not related to the *Tarzan* airframes, and that the issues were not typical. The video of the one flight made at the end of the week at Camp Roberts proved that point.

Having petitioned the Lord, Shawn and the Theiss team determined to accept whatever His answer might be and in His good time. Some days passed and the Theiss work force busied themselves with the cleaning of the office/shop complex, and the mowing and trimming of twelve acres of grass air strip and taxiways; all while praying for God's favor in this situation.

Shawn himself was spending as much time as possible with his wife, Charlene, and their now three children. Lately he had been in the shop and on the road for too long of periods of time. His two young sons and ten-year-old daughter, Josette, had their daddy needs too! So, between his involvement with upkeep of the Theiss facility, the ongoing air force bird development program, and church activities, he found time for boating, playing, and roller skating. There was too little time for rest—an ongoing concern for Richard and Hope. And then it came!

The huge door of opportunity was starting to swing open again. "Hey Dad!" Shawn, at the computer, called out to the one sanding and varnishing three more Tarzans on the assembly line. "Take a look at this!"

The tone of Shawn's voice moved Richard, with haste, toward the focus of his attention. There, on the screen, was the most complete answer to the Theiss team's pointed prayer requests.

"Dear Mr. Shawn Theiss," opened the communication. "The NAVAIR officer in command has reviewed all data related to the Theiss/BAI contract and has determined that the events that have caused the delays in acceptance of the UAV System are not typical and are understandable." The opening paragraph caused Richard to shout, "Praise God!" As both men read on, the suggested arrangements for continuing the contract were offered. Payments would be made as both planes completed their acceptance flights. Simple enough for the NAVAIR, not so for Theiss.

The return to California would depend on Tom Zets' availability. To lock him into a time slot would first require Tom to make time arrangements on his end first, then there would need to be air travel arrangements. Work still had to be done on the plane that had up-ended; the replacement of the engine, prop, and broken exhaust stack were still required. Add this all in with the setting out of a new schedule for the training of the BAI pilots—it was becoming apparent that moving forward would be costly. However, the bottom line was the blessing of being able to have time to test fly, fly the acceptance, and complete instructional flights for the BAI pilots. A "Wahoo!" and "Thank you

Father!" for Shawn Theiss and company. The really big door was really wide open.

The month of September 2010 not only ushered in the fresh air of the fall season, but also an air of accomplishment—not that the demons were giving up on their diversions, but even they can be slow to learn that, when all is said and done, our Lord reigns.

As Shawn set up for his return to the California air strip, he learned that during the first of a two week period, the base had double booked the test site and the hangar needed for the Theiss preflight activities would not be available. How could this be? Would he have to take the planes off-base while working on them? What about the fact that their mission was secret? Was this of no concern? The answer to all of the above was that the base would be conducting priority training maneuvers in that area and Shawn would have to shift his preflight activities elsewhere. The Theiss team prayed for God to send someone in authority with understanding and the desire to help.

Shawn flew out to the air strip with no indication of how God would answer, but he had a firm belief that the blessing was already there ahead of him.

Early the next morning, Shawn had already planned the steps for relocating the preflight activities. Still hopeful for a blessing, he emailed one last attempt for use of the needed hangar space and then drove less than a mile to a U-Haul location. Here, he rented a truck large enough to transport both planes back to a storage area in which to conduct the required repairs and preflight work.

Having made a few stops along the way to Camp Roberts for the items he would need to transfer the planes, Shawn found that the normal road from the main gate to the air strip was not available to him. Ongoing base maneuvers had closed that access. Surely God was aware of the back road Shawn found himself driving on. Surely He knew that the washboard ruts would destroy the two aircraft Shawn would soon be carrying back to the U-Haul location. "Dear Lord, this is not how things were supposed to be turning out."

Sure enough, the long rough and dusty road did end up close to the paved air strip. The airfield was swarming with uniforms and suits. Having parked the U-Haul truck next to the ground control station, Shawn set about for the transfer of the two UAV's. The interesting shape of the craft in their folded configuration caught the eyes of two nearby officers. They asked Shawn about his activities. After his brief explanation one of the officers offered, "Oh, so you're the fellow who sent the email this morning!" Continued conversation revealed the fact that Shawn was indeed talking to the officer in command of the training exercise that was taking priority of the facility.

However, he was so impressed with both the craft and Shawn's manner that the officer stated that Shawn could not only work at the facility while the exercise was ongoing, but he could even do so in the very hangar that was originally to be used by Theiss Aviation.

As Shawn flatly stated in a call to his VP, "Dad, He answered again in the eleventh hour." A lesson reaffirmed—you never give up but wait on the Lord.

It was most evident at this point that the Satanic ones were livid. The battle in the unseen realm raged on. Initial test flights were completed, and the team began to step through the acceptance flight criteria. After successful down range flights and the climb to ten thousand feet of altitude (at nearly seven-hundred feet per minute) were completed, the engine again presented a serious problem.

The next acceptance step was the endurance flight. About two hours into the endurance flight, the engine seized (stopped completely). Although BAI was treated to an unscheduled, dead stick landing (in which the craft handled perfectly), the ensuing delay was not welcomed. The engine was once again pulled and shipped back to the manufacturer for inspection and repair. The culprit in the engine was initially determined to be the bearings, not Theiss manufactured equipment, but still not well.

Of deep concern over the next two weeks of flight testing and the training of BAI pilots was the unwelcomed seizure of the second engine on the second airframe; now both engines had seized in flight. It was at this very crucial time in the completion of the project that Shawn displayed what Richard referred to as "the Christian tender heart." The outcry of all who had to do with the contract was "Change engine companies, fast!" After all, now it was the Theiss Aviation firm's reputation at stake, and it wasn't looking good.

"Dad," Shawn confided, "I'm sure that the engine company, being small as we are, has used any money we have paid them to take care of their bills. To terminate their contract at this time could be devastating to them, and possibly even more delaying to this project!" This was true.

But what successful businessman would consider those points at this point in time? Shawn would. Perhaps Shawn's mode of thinking was the reason the Theiss firm was (some twenty years into the aircraft business) not much larger than it was at its beginning. In all of that time, Richard was sure that not one night of sleep had been lost by any of the staff due to an overcharge or unfair treatment of a client or a government office. Indeed, many were the deals offered that were something less than the shade of truthfulness. For Shawn, it was black or white; he simply could not pull the rug out from under his engine supplier.

Once again, Shawn would rely on his Heavenly Father to supply the needed time to complete the time-overrun contract. Once again, his ever hearing God supplied his request. However, there would be no more money to fill the till (at this time) until all training flights were accomplished.

Another intense month of activity lay ahead—the pulling and shipping of the engines, rescheduling of needed airport facility dates, and of course, arrangements for pilot Tom to return yet again. Remembering the words of Jesus, "Without me, you can do nothing," Shawn and his staff were in constant prayer and trust.

On Thursday, October 25, 2010, Shawn and his wife flew to the California military base for the set up of what would be the final thrust in the NAVAIR contract. Tom would join Shawn on the following Wednesday to train the BAI pilots over the next two days. As usual, time would be the critical factor, and everything would need to go virtually flawless to accomplish everything within the short timeframe. This was to be the last chance to complete the contract. If not successfully completed, the contract would be cancelled, and Theiss Aviation would be in a heap of financial debt. It was all or nothing at this point, and it was all in God's hands.

ALL THINGS CONSIDERED

Business wise, nation wise, and world wise, it was evident that Shawn was living in the most critical of times. For Theiss Aviation, it seemed that the ensuing circumstances were a test of faith and hope. At the same time, the United States was facing the most important election of governmental officers in its entire history, and the world itself seemed poised for international disaster.

Did someone say wars and rumors of wars, natural disasters, lawlessness, and lovers of pleasure rather than God? Each daily newscast, along with newspapers and magazines, were validating the things foretold in the Christian Bible. All things considered, would there be many more surprises facing humanity? Not for the Christian.

For Theiss Aviation, God was always there at the right time and with the right answers. For the Nation, no matter how the elections were to turn out, the momentum of God's timing for the last days would continue to their completion. For the World, the day for the gathering of God's true *born again* believers was next in the line of completely accurate Biblical prophecies.

Even with all of the above at hand, Shawn and the Theiss Team would continue to provide the people of our nation with flying things of every size, shape, and description as required by the Department of Defense.

This, while preparing themselves and their loved ones to be taken up to meet Jesus in the air (referred to as the Rapture).

Sound strange? Unrealistic? Impossible?

For those of you readers who doubt this biblical fact, I'm afraid that you're in for one great big *Surprise, Surprise*!

LIST OF ACRONYMS

AFRL – Air Force Research Laboratory

BAI – Bernstien Aerospace Incorporated

BAI – Brandes Associates Incorporated

CIA – Counter Intelligence Agency

DARPA – Defense Advanced Research Projects Agency

FAA – Federal Aviation Administration

FBI – Federal Bureau of Investigation

NASA – National Air and Space Administration

NRL – Naval Research Laboratory

STOL – Short Take Off and Landing

TAI – Theiss Aviation Incorporated

USA – United States of America